Thatchers and thatching

Thatchers and thatching

JUDY NASH

B.T. Batsford Ltd · London

For Harry, with love

First published 1991

© Judy Nash, 1991

ISBN 0 7134 6458 5

Typeset by Best-set Typesetter Ltd

Printed and Bound by
Courier International Limited, East Kilbride

For the Publisher
B.T. Batsford Limited
4 Fitzhardinge Street
London w1h 0ah

A catalogue record for this book is
available from the British Library

Contents

Sources of illustrations

The photographs in this book are reproduced by courtesy of the following:

18 – Landmark Trust; *26, 127* – John Husband; *29* – Manx Museum; *38* – Jonathan MacDonald; *43* – Guy Gale; *54* – Peter Brugge; *68(top)*, *176*, *177* – Ian Sumner; *89* – Mrs E. Winn; *93, 179* – Fairclough Homes Ltd; *145* – Yetminster PCC & Hundred of Yetminster History Soc.; *153* – Mrs N. Lucy; *163* – Western Gazette Co. Ltd; *164* – Colin Hoare; *170* – Torbay News Agency; *171*, *172* – Rural Development Commission; *173, 174* – Thatching Advisory Service. The remaining photographs are from the Nash and Garrett collections.

I should like to thank the Butser Ancient Farm Project Trust and Queen Elizabeth Country Park and The Weald and Downland Open Air Museum for inviting us to take photographs of their reconstructed buildings; Abbotsbury Swannery for inviting us to photograph the reed cutting; and Carl Saunders and St Mary's Middle School, Puddletown, for sending information and plans for their reconstructed Saxon longhouse.

Acknowledgements

My warmest thanks go to the Master Thatchers and their apprentices who have allowed us to interrupt their work; the retired Master Thatchers who have related their family histories; the staff of the Weald and Downland Open Air Museum; the Butser Ancient Farm Project Trust and Queen Elizabeth Country Park; Julia Abel Smith of the Landmark Trust; the Manx Museum; the Finch Foundry Museum; Jonathan MacDonald of the Skye Museum of Island Life; John A. Spence for the Ancient Monuments of Orkney; Thatching Officer Peter Brockett; Mrs H. Edmunds and the Rural Development Commission; Charles Cator of the British Reed Growers' Association; Christopher White and the National Society of Master Thatchers; the Thatching Advisory Service; the National Society of Master Thatchers; Mike Pearson and Swanherd John Fair of Abbotsbury Swannery; R.S.P.B. Warden, D. Ireland; Mr Simon Wingfield Digby and Sherborne Castle Estate; the Forestry Commission; the Royal Society for Nature Conservation; Fairclough Homes Ltd; Balfour Beatty Homes; Dorset County Record Office; Dorset County Reference Library; Yeovil Library; Yeovil Museum; Ricardo Ltd (building contractors), Guildford Library; The Jenner Museum; St Fagan's Welsh Folk Museum; and Pentagram.

I am also greatly indebted to the many individuals who have contributed in some way; for their enthusiasm, anecdotes and ideas and for inviting us to see and photograph their thatched properties. Special thanks to sparmaker Graeme Coombs; thatchers Pete Hindle, Ron Gosney, Stephen Pope, Alan Grey-Hodder, Guy Gale, Alan Fooks, the Farman family, Tony Cottrell, Harold Wright, Peter Brugge, Jonathan MacDonald, William Tegetmeier; reed-cutter Dick Dalley; importer Peter Grimley; hurdlemakers Montague and Sidney Donald Davis; Mr and Mrs H.W. Perry of Perry's Cider Mills; John Husband, the Partridge family, Len Hoskins and all branches of the Garrett, Gray and Hunt families. Finally, I want to thank my husband, Harry, for his help, ideas, photographic skills and many hours spent in the darkroom and also my father Master Thatcher Simon Garrett for the inspiration for this book, for his patience and enthusiasm for his craft and for his willingness to share his reminiscences with others.

Introduction

Everyone appreciates a newly thatched roof with its golden coat shining in the sunlight but sadly, few people consider the thatcher himself, without whose skill and perseverance, even in times of hardship, agricultural depression, drought and blizzard, we should have lost this rare breed of man and thus the cottages we so admire today.

Not all thatchers survived the times of hardship, and we may yet lose many more of the established thatching families, steeped in centuries of tradition, but those last members who are approaching retirement age have the satisfaction of knowing that the resurgence of interest in their craft will take it safely through to the twenty-first century.

Today, the thatcher is a businessman as well as a craftsman and has had to come to terms with a new, fiercely competitive world that his thatching forbears could not have visualized. Little more than 20 years ago their wet weather occupation would have been sparmaking in the cart shed until their backs ached and they prayed for the rain to stop. Today's thatchers, on a wet day, are more likely to be found balancing their books, completing their tax returns and typing estimates for prospective customers.

However, not everything has changed, for the basic principles of securing the thatch to the roof have remained unaltered for centuries. There has been a slow evolution of method, materials, tools and style but the pace of change did not accelerate with the Industrial and Agricultural Revolutions but rather progressed steadily to cope with the demands of each era. It was not until the mid-1950s, by which time the combine harvester was a common sight in even the smallest fields, that the thatcher felt his livelihood was threatened. By this time many traditional thatching families had been split apart by two World Wars, increased travel due to the expansion of the railway network and a new outlook that made the surviving younger generation of thatchers contribute somewhat less to the stability of their rural communities.

The disbanding of large estates, crippled by death duties and land tax, removed the day-to-day workload that many thatchers had relied on. Other estate owners, disheartened by the deaths of their heirs in two World Wars, no longer found thatch desirable for lodges, keepers' cottages and summerhouses; the houseparties had dwindled and few were left to appreciate the picturesque and rustic creations of the last century.

Farmers too were veering away from thatched barns, implement sheds and eventually even the building of ricks, which had provided the bulk of thatchers' summer work and been a reliable source of income.

When farmers welcomed the combine harvester into their fields the thatchers saw their basic material chopped into short, unusable lengths. Even if the farmers had persevered with their reapers and binders the new, shorter wheat varieties with pith-filled stems proved unsuitable for the thatchers' needs. In some areas marsh reed also became hard to obtain as well as the means of fixing the thatch to the roof.

The thatching spar – a bent hairpin of a variety of pliable woods like hazel and willow – was becoming scarce because estates were no longer managing their woodland on traditional lines. Prime timber and not the products of the underwood occupied owners' minds as a sure source of income, and grant-aided conifer plantations were soon to replace hazel coppices. Traditional woodsmen themselves were no longer available to continue the traditional crafts; the demand for hazel products had fallen and post-war increases in the cost of living had turned sons away from following in their fathers' footsteps when higher wages could be earned elsewhere.

In 1851 over 800 Devon thatchers had declared this their full-time occupation but the numbers subsequently plummeted from an estimated post-war number of 800 nationwide to little more than 300 by 1950. After the Second World War, help came at last from the Rural Industries Bureau, and regional Master Thatchers Associations. These were intended to support the few remaining craftsmen: give advice (general and legal) on the many problems that confronted them, boost their flagging spirits by providing them with opportunities to meet socially and help find sources of tools and materials. Many Master Thatchers Associations have recently celebrated their fortieth anniversary and show an increased membership, especially in the younger age range.

To 'Thaec' once meant to cover a roof with any material. Today the word thatch is only associated with those grass and cereal crops that can provide a waterproof covering to the roof, and some are more popular than others. Regional variations are less clearly defined than even 30 years ago, when marsh reed was confined to the estuary areas where it was cultivated, combed wheat reed or Devon reed extended through the West Country and long straw – a variation using randomly applied stems of the wheat crop – found everywhere, whereas Norfolk reed extended little beyond the neighbouring counties and imported reed was virtually unknown.

Today the customer looks at the economics as much as the style and may show little regard for the vernacular. The life expectancy of marsh reed can be double that of combed wheat reed and is said to be four times that of long straw, although traditional long-straw thatchers disagree. Thatch is no longer the poor man's roofing material but competes with tiles and slates. The thatcher's time is not cheap, so prospective customers opt for the longest lasting material they can afford. Hence it is not uncommon to find Norfolk reed in Devon, Turkish reed in Dorset and combed wheat reed applied in the long-straw style in areas where long straw once predominated.

The 1980s saw the first thatched house at the Ideal Homes Exhibition, a thatched cottage at the National Garden Festival and the first thatched executive homes. The upsurge of interest was confirmed and throughout the country new houses began to appear with thatched roofs. Corrugated iron sheets applied for economy earlier this century have been ripped off and replaced by thatch, and countless country cottages have been renovated and turned into the ideal of the new country cottage dwellers. The economy of the application of a patch seems to have become a thing of the past and now it is more usual to find a complete new covering of thatch.

The life of the thatching man through the ages has not been considered before. Although thatchers are often thought to have suffered most in the recent post-war period their survival throughout history has been precarious on many occasions.

The thatcher today is a businessman with less time to experiment with the allied crafts (such as hurdle- and sparmaking) of his predecessors but talking to him reveals his underlying feelings are the same. His appreciation of his countryside, his natural instinct for shape and what is just 'right' for a particular roof shines through. He fiercely defends his craft, interprets his skill to the best of his ability (and is proud of the result) and fortunately has retained his sense of humour.

Today the thatching woman is not such a rarity and, like the thatching man, often finds the craft a way of expressing her artistic talents without the restrictions of an office, enclosed environment. Dorset thatcher Pete Hindle said in 1989 with new found conviction, 'As long as there is a thatched roof there will be a thatcher to thatch it;' and no doubt he will be proved right, as the increasing number of young Master Thatchers approach the future with confidence, having changed with the times and succeeded in carving a niche for themselves against almost impossible odds.

NB Both metric and imperial measurements are used in the text; these reflect the origin and/or date of the source material. (1 acre = 0.4 hectares; 1 ton = 0.98 tonnes.)

1

A craft is born

Who the earliest thatchers were we shall never know but we can be certain they have existed since man first built himself a house, over 12,000 years ago. We do not know their names, thoughts, preferences or even their burial places but thanks to their persistence in developing a sound thatching style at an early date thatch has remained in use despite competition from tiles and slates.

The oldest thatched houses to survive date from the thirteenth century but from archaeological excavations we can form a good idea of the shape and structure of even older buildings and often the total absence of fragments of roofing material in the ground indicates that these buildings were thatched. Many roofs were surprisingly large, too vast for a self-sufficient farmer to have completed on his own in a reasonable length of time. To help him he would have selected those men who had shown their skill in creating a long-lasting weatherproof roof that withstood the force of winter gales and needed only periodic maintenance. The first thatchers had arrived.

Early man learnt quickly, for his life was a constant battle for survival. His basic requirements were food and shelter, quickly followed by an appreciation of warmth and

thus fire. On abandoning his nomadic life in favour of establishing settled farming communities he experimented with the wide variety of roofing materials growing around him. Grasses, rushes, heather and broom were soon supplemented by straw, the by-product of his early cereal crop, and although this crop realized only small quantities of straw and grain compared to the amount produced by modern intensive farming methods, they were sufficient for his needs.

Thatch was not only readily available but also the lightest form of roofing material. It was easy to transport the short distance from the field to where it was required and the roof structure needed to be of only the simplest construction. Large rafters were unnecessary and small, uncleft hedge poles could form the basis for an adequate roof, that with careful maintenance could survive several centuries. Where timber was scarce and either had to be brought into the area or ferried to islands by boat this factor was of prime importance. In coastal regions maximum use was made of driftwood washed up on to the beach.

Roofs were made steeply pitched to shed water quickly from the outside of the thatch.

The shallower the angle of the roof timbers the quicker the rain would have penetrated to the interior of the building and today's thatched buildings retain a steeply pitched roof for the same reason.

Greek and Roman scholars recorded descriptions of Iron Age thatched houses but early textbooks conveyed the impression that primitive man survived in flimsy shelters that were without skill in their construction. Archaeological excavations of the remains of massive thatched round-houses have proved this was far from the case. Not all houses were large and obviously the early thatcher learnt his skills on the roofs of these smaller buildings.

Early roofs may have appeared roughly finished, with thatch thrown on in untidy heaps and fastened by a variety of means but the thatcher soon realized the importance of the spar. The recent discovery of wattle hurdles, dating from Neolithic times, in the peat bogs of Somerset proves that woodland management was practised at a very early date. Men who possessed the skill to make hurdles similar to those sold in garden centres today would have been aware of the many uses of the hazel and willow that grew prolifically around them. Baskets, useful implements and containers were woven from the pliable stems and no doubt it was quickly realized that a simple hooked peg or bent hairpin shape would fasten thatch more securely to the roof.

Large round-houses were common in Iron Age settlements and disprove the theory that thatching was at a very primitive stage of development at the time. It might have been possible to make a waterproof roof covering on a small hut without previous experience but not on round-houses that had a diameter of up to 55 feet (17 metres). Archaeological excavations uncover exactly where the post holes were positioned in the earth to hold the supporting timbers, and reconstructions show the massive size of these huts. Iron Age man would not have

tolerated a large roof that was labour intensive to construct if it had immediately proved impossible to make it watertight. Such houses were constructed over a long period of history so the design must have proved satisfactory or the constructions would not have been repeated. They also point to the thatcher being in existence as an independent craftsman. Roofs that take up to six tons of thatching material to coat them could not have been thatched by one self-sufficient farming family. Their other routine farming tasks would have occupied most of the daylight hours and it would have been sensible to use the skills of the man or men who had proved themselves capable of thatching their own small huts in a weatherproof and long-lasting style.

The Celts must always have appreciated the need to prepare for the winter months and this was a time-consuming process. Any way of saving time would have been utilized to the full and there would have been a constant supply of work for the thatcher. Winter fodder was scarce and it was essential to store what had been harvested in such a way that it was palatable when retrieved from the rick. Grain pits would probably have been lined with a wattle of hazel and a thatched canopy would have given greater protection. Animal shelters were thatched too, and perhaps the early thatcher filled in any spare winter hours by producing woven fencing and cutting himself sufficient supplies of spar gads for the coming year.

Round-houses were popular in Ireland where artificial islands (crannogs) were built in lakes and bogs to form the foundations for a small community. Peat, brushwood, rushes and logs were some of the materials used to create the platform on which thatched round-houses were built and then surrounded by a perimeter fence. Over 200 of these settlements have been discovered as well as several thousand ring-forts constructed on dry land. A replica crannog

Butser ancient farm reconstruction, Queen Elizabeth country park, Hampshire.

Round structures were the ideal shape to withstand winter weather. This small round-house was reconstructed at the Butser Ancient Farm site in Hampshire

has been built at Craggaunowen, in County Clare, where the circular house took more than ten tons of mud to coat the wattle walls and 3,600 bales of rushes to thatch the roof.

Thatched Saxon houses and a communal hall were reconstructed on the site of a village at West Stow in Suffolk that was abandoned around AD 650 for a more suitable site nearby. As house styles evolved there were many opportunities for the thatcher to practise his craft and develop an individual style.

As communities grew larger little thought was given to overall planning or to the

design or siting of new properties, and fire became an accepted risk. Most major towns suffered severely on several occasions and although the cause of the fire cannot always be attributed to the thatch, there is no doubt that flames spread quickly from house to house. The days of the urban thatcher were numbered, as an increasing number of authorities banned new thatched properties.

There were many devastating fires in the Middle Ages. Fires in London are recorded in 1077, 1087, 1135, 1136 and 1161. Canterbury, Exeter and Winchester also suffered in 1161 and Winchester again in

1180. Glastonbury's major fire was in 1184, Chichester's in 1187, Worcester's in 1202 and Chester suffered on two occasions in 1140 and 1180. A large part of Blandford Forum was destroyed in 1278.

Not all fires were accidental and Beaminster's first fire on Palm Sunday 1644 was started by soldiers of the Royalist Army of Prince Maurice who are believed to have deliberately fired their muskets into the thatched roofs. In two hours 144 of the estimated 200 dwelling houses were burnt out. In 1645 the Parliamentary Army was at Beaminster, and Joshua Sprigge the historian records:

The train and most of the foot quartered on the top of an hill; some laid in Beaminster town, a place of the pityfalest spectacle that man can behold, hardly an house left not consumed with fire.[1]

Less than 40 years later a second fire, on 18 June 1684, caused such devastation that less combustible roofing materials were chosen for the new town. Unfortunately, this decision meant no fresh work for Beaminster's thatcher.

Butser ancient farm reconstruction, Queen Elizabeth country park, Hampshire.

The skills of the Iron Age thatchers can only be appreciated from reconstructions such as this, that used almost five tonnes of wheat reed and 200 trees

London authorities encouraged the building of stone houses with stone party walls and laid down conditions for roofing in the city at a very early date. At the London Assize of 1212 it was ordered:

whosoever wishes to build, let him take care, as he loveth himself and his goods, that he roof not with reed, nor rush, straw, nor stubble, but with tile only, or shingle, or boards, or, if it may be, with lead, or plastered straw within the city and portsoken. Also that all houses which till now are covered with reed or rush, which can be plastered, let them be plastered within eight days, and let those which shall not be so plastered within the term be demolished by the alderman and lawful men of the venue.[2]

This Ordnance was only partly successful and not all aldermen carried out its ruling to the letter. Other towns followed suit theoretically but in many cases the law was never enforced and later examples of thatched buildings close to town centres still survive today. As time passed natural decay saw the removal of most of the primitive dwellings and more fireproof materials took their place.

In 1264 Simon de Montfort, in his efforts to overthrow the throne, planned to make use of thatched roofs, that still remained in large enough quantities for him to think his plan would succeed. Chickens were to be released with flaming brands attached to their legs which (he thought) would quickly lead to the city being destroyed. The plan did not succeed and may not even have been attempted.

Some cities were late in passing laws regarding the use of thatch and in Norwich the tiling of roofs was not compulsory until 1509. The whitewashing of thatch in less densely populated areas was felt to be a sufficient fire deterrent and this method was practised in Wales until this century. The preference for bricks and tiles by the prosperous yeoman farmers saw the demise of thatch in some counties of the south and

south-east, but in 1610 Bishop Hall was still able to observe

of one baye's bredth, God wot! a silly cote,
Whose thatched sparres are furr'd with sluttish soot,
A whole inch thick, shining like black-moor's brows[3]

Perhaps some fires were due to the excess soot catching fire and not the thatch beneath it!

After the Fire of London in 1666, thatch was finally forbidden in most British towns. Earlier rulings seem to have been disregarded in London when theatres such as the Globe, the Swan and the Rose were built. The first Globe theatre, built in 1599, burned down in 1613 when a wad fired from a stage cannon during a performance of *Henry VIII* set the thatch alight. The newly excavated Rose Theatre, built in 1587, shows indications of having been thatched and a sketch that has survived of the Swan Theatre shows a thatched roof.[4]

Some thatched villages disappeared before this date and the cause can often be directly attributed to the Black Death. Bubonic plague arrived on ships docking at Melcombe Regis, Dorset in 1348 and in two years had wiped out up to half of the country's population. Some villages were left with too few able-bodied men to survive, as was the case at Hangleton, Sussex where only two cottages remained by 1428 and were abandoned soon afterwards.

The thatcher who survived the plague often found his livelihood removed, as too few villagers had survived to need his skills. For the first time travel was essential to put the thatcher in contact with communities that had lost their own craftsmen, but once established he could demand higher wages. In 1251/2 at Downton, Wiltshire a thatcher was paid wages of 6s 4d for thatching an ox-shed in straw (the total construction cost to the owner being 12s 5d) and 16s for thatching a new barn.[5] His income was

Hangleton cottage at the Weald and Downland Open Air Museum. A reconstruction based on the deserted village of Hangleton on the Downs above Hove, Sussex. *The inset shows a close-up of the smoke-hole.*

The ability of thatch to blend into its surroundings is evident here. The smoke-hole illustrates a style of thatch continued in some eastern counties today where the gable end is elaborately rolled and sparred down

considerably more than the recommended shilling a week for labourers of the fourteenth century.

The choice of a rectangular structure had its advantages: more head room at the gable end led to second storeys being constructed, and the straight walls and corners made the space easier to furnish and divide into rooms. This led to the development of a different thatching style. A method of securing thatch at the corners of the eaves was developed as well as a rolled edge around the smoke-holes or 'gablets' that encouraged smoke to filter through to the outside. About the year 1300 small, simple cottages cost between 12 and 25 shillings to build and the thatcher was often paid four pence a day for his labours.[6] Many houses were not substantial in construction and must have suffered the same fate as the medieval village of Conisborough, Yorkshire, said to have been blown away in a gale.

The visual impact of reconstructed buildings often leaves a more lasting impression of man's early achievements and skills than any textbook can but not everyone appreciates such structures. Conservationists spent a year restoring 15 acres of wilderness near Chepstow at Llanvair Discoed, 800 feet (244 metres) above the Severn Estuary to how it looked 350 years ago but the local council preferred derelict ruins surrounded by undergrowth, and Gloucestershire farmer Mr Stuart

Peachey awaits an enforcement order for the demolition of his reconstructed seventeenth-century thatched cottage.[7]

Other reconstructions are welcomed and planning permission was granted readily in 1990 for a thatched Anglo-Saxon hall house to be reconstructed by St Mary's Middle School at Puddletown, Dorset for educational purposes. Information has been researched from archaeological excavations at Churchdown, Hampshire. A close link has been formed between the school, the

Purton Green Farmhouse, Stansfield, Suffolk.

Rurally situated Purton Green Farmhouse was not affected by the legislature of the towns. It was an important dwelling when it was constructed in the thirteenth century

A hall from Boarhunt, north-west of Portsmouth, Hampshire, photographed on its new site, 1989.

This is the smallest base-cruck hall yet discovered, and now stands in the Weald and Downland Open Air Museum

RSPB and local thatchers. Reed will be supplied for the project from the 1990 harvest at the reed beds adjacent to the Radipole Lake Reserve and thatchers will advise on techniques. The project can only create a greater understanding of the craftsmen's skills and an appreciation of thatch by the pupils who will be involved in the work.

Very few houses have survived from before the Tudor period. One of the oldest to do so on its original site is Purton Green Farmhouse at Stansfield, Suffolk, which was built in the middle of the thirteenth century. It must have been built for a wealthy farmer and is a good example of a timber-framed aisled hall house. It was a large substantial dwelling for its age but despite its size and importance it was converted into tenements and had become derelict by 1969 when it was rescued by the Landmark Trust. When it was built there were no chimney stacks but the two-storey house did pose new problems for the thatcher in the shape of a seventeenth-century chimney stack, inserted no doubt at a time when the roof was re-thatched. Considerable sympathetic restoration work has secured the future of Purton Green. The appreciation of such early styles has led to many cottages becoming listed dwellings that will need the services of the thatcher at regular intervals in the future. Houses like this gave man the desired headroom that the early huts had not, but meant that for the first time the thatcher needed a long ladder to reach the eaves. No doubt he then stepped on to a series of small roofing ladders held in place by spikes pushed deep into the thatch, similar to those in use today.

The deterioration of the climate in the fourteenth century probably affected the fenland and the fen edge more than anywhere else in the country. There was a strict regime for reed cutting on the fens at this time. Other lowlying areas such as the Somerset Levels disappeared under water. Not only was 1316 the first year of the great famine but also a year of unprecedented rainfall. Places that had never been flooded before disappeared beneath the encroaching water. Supplies of thatch would have been in short supply for many of these years when crops failed, and would have led to any

Hymerford House, North Coker, Somerset.

Thatch was considered suitable for the manor house as well as the cottage when Hymerford House was built

Spring Cottage, Chetnole, Dorset, 1989.

Some new timbers and a fresh coat of over two tons of Aquila combed wheat reed ensures a safe future for Spring Cottage, built almost 500 years before the date of this photography

available materials being used for patching roofs rather than new work.

As the population slowly recovered from the effects of the Black Death communities regrouped. The break with tradition led to freedom to experiment with a variety of roof styles.

A full hip-ended thatched hall from Boarhunt, Hampshire was well constructed in the fifteenth century and despite later additions it was possible to gain enough information about its base-cruck construction to re-build it at the Weald and Downland Open Air Museum in its original form. The absence of a second storey and chimney stack made it an easy style for the thatcher and the full hip end meant a continuous line of thatch all around the building – a sensible design that was unlikely to suffer from gale damage.

Although the style of houses was constantly changing, influenced not only by fashion but also by the purse of the individual, thatch remained in abundance, supplying rural thatchers with sufficient work when coupled with rick and farm thatching. A team of thatchers probably tackled the large roof of Hymerford House, North Coker, Somerset, named after the family that occupied it in the fifteenth and sixteenth centuries. In the seventeenth century the famous navigator and explorer Captain William Dampier was born there. Stone built and rendered, with some attractive Gothic windows, the exterior appears little altered apart from the addition of guttering. Thatched manor houses were more common at this date. Hayes Barton Manor House near Sidmouth in Devon is large but followed the vernacular style of

cob walls topped with thatch when it was built in the sixteenth century. Not all thatched manor houses have survived. Thoughtless modernization cannot always be blamed for their disappearance for some were victims of natural disasters, such as Berne Manor House in Dorset, which was struck by lightning in 1926 and totally destroyed.

Thatched cottages from this time were not nearly as large as Hymerford House. At Misterton, Somerset, 30 new cottages were built between 1556 and the end of that century. Many such cottages were of local

'The Muntings', Yetminster, Dorset.

Cleft roof timbers are held together by oak pegs and wedges in this house, built in 1540. Some needed replacing in 1989 before the thatchers could complete their work

Colliers Cottage, Fontmell Magna, Dorset.

The vernacular style has been adhered to. Closely clipped marsh reed would alter the character of this long-straw cottage

importance and housed prosperous yeoman farmers. Spring Cottage borders the River Wriggle at Chetnole, Dorset and served its owners well. It was not until 1989 that some of the original roof timbers needed replacing. Sympathetic restoration ensured that as many original features were preserved as possible, especially the wattle surround of the original smoke-hole. With a complete new coat of combed wheat, Aquila reed and sound timbers this listed building will need no further attention until the ridge needs replacing in about seven years time. Although scaffolding was erected it is obvious there is little height from ground level to the eaves.

On opening the roof of 'The Muntings', Yetminster, for repair work in 1989, a large chimney-breast was uncovered as well as the fact that a purlin (horizontal support beam), first discovered almost a century ago, had been broken and covered by the shaped board from a waggon. The exterior coat had shown no sign of subsidence which proves the thatchers claim that 'The thatch holds the roof up'! Over three tons of Aquila reed was used by thatchers Ron Gosney and Mark Coombs who drew attention to the fact that the roof construction contained no nails. Oak pegs and wedges as well as roughly hewn timber proved the age of the cottage which had last been thatched 30 years before. As storm clouds gathered the thatchers worked on and were successful in completing the work before rain fell.

Some cottages made extensive use of

driftwood for both roof timbers and temporary repairs. If driftwood was not available villagers were not averse to plundering wrecks. The cottage of Abbotsbury Swannery Decoyman, 'Dick' Dalley, was found to have teak roof timbers when the roof was stripped ready for re-thatching in recent years. Teak would almost certainly have come from the deck planking of a ship washed ashore along the storm-lashed Chesil Bank, on the Dorset coast. It had served well, for it had resisted woodworm and was as sound as the day it was acquired. Individual timbers that needed to be replaced to keep a ship seaworthy were usually sufficiently sound to be incorporated in a house. Some timbers were sold from old dismantled ships for this purpose but others were taken as patterns to areas of oak forest for new pieces to be cut, and then left behind.

From the mid-seventeenth century the thatcher had had the opportunity to experiment with various styles of thatch on different roof shapes. Thereafter, as ceilings became more common there was no longer a need for elaborate roof timbers and it may have been at this time that the owner of the

Woolcombe, Dorset.

Woolcombe Hayes is a mixture of styles: a combed wheat-reed roof at the front and marsh reed at the back

House from Walderton, Sussex, rebuilt at the Weald and Downland Open Air Museum.

The outer façade can be deceptive; this seventeenth-century exterior conceals a fifteenth-century timber-framed building

thatched house (but not of the poorer thatched hovels) turned his attention to the appearance of his roof and exterior walls. The design and appearance of houses was also affected by the window tax of 1695 which lasted through the eighteenth century, and a tax on bricks in 1784 which was not removed until 1850. Many house owners reconsidered their choice of materials at this time.

Thatch was not restricted to dwelling houses; as well as its many agricultural uses it was also the chosen roofing material for most early churches, many inns and commercial premises. At Gwaensgor, North Wales, St Magdalene's Church was rebuilt by the Normans and thatched, replacing an earlier timber-framed thatched church. When a heavier slate roof replaced the thatched one short purlins and an extra rafter had to be inserted between each pair of couples in the roof structure to support the extra weight.

Although Cornwall does not abound with thatched properties, a simple coat of thatch was the chosen roofing material for the Quaker Meeting House at 'Come-to-Good', a name derived from the Cornish 'House in

Come-to-Good, Cornwall.

This Quaker Meeting House may seem an unusual building today but it typifies a practical design that would have been used by thatchers and builders everywhere when it was built in 1709/10

the Coombe', which was built in 1709–10. It was originally a plain rectangular building measuring 20 × 27 feet (6.1 × 8.2 metres) inside with whitewashed cob walls and an open-timbered thatched roof erected at a total cost of £68 18s 3d. A catslide roof has been added to cover the adjoining stable and in 1717 an interior gallery cost £15 10s. A thatched porch was added to the west side in 1967.

Low roofs with little height from ground level to eaves were chosen for a wide variety of reasons; they not only suited the thatcher, who could easily reach the roof, but also the purse of the builder as less materials were needed. These were not the only reasons, for

climatic factors often dictated the safe ridge height to withstand exceptional weather conditions.

The Decoyman's House at Abbotsbury Swannery, Dorset was constructed to suit the extreme weather conditions of the area behind the Chesil Bank. Its rectangular shape, presenting its half-hipped narrowest end to the direction of the worst coastal weather was not coincidental. The roofing material was the local 'spear' water reed grown in the adjacent reed beds. Most of the original cottage, which lies below sea level, was destroyed by a freak tidal wave which submerged it to a depth of almost 23 feet (7 metres). A commemorative marker pole indicates the enormity of the situation. The Great Storm, as it was called, hit the coast on 23 November 1824 and the waves crashed over the Chesil beach raising the level of the Lagoon by 20 feet (6.1 metres), flooding houses and drowning many in their homes. At least three ships were wrecked that night and one was washed right over the bank of pebbles. The *Western Gazette* reported 'tempest heavy with more frightful terrors is scarcely within the memory of man'.

The cottage has been restored and now houses an appropriate display of wildlife with the present Decoyman preferring to live in a thatched cottage considerably higher above sea level in the village. High tides are not unknown today and in January 1990 the Decoyman was able to row his boat over the top of the reed beds.

Thatched taverns adorned most village streets in counties where thatch prevailed. Many were small to suit village needs and thatch had good insulating properties which meant warmth was maintained by no more than an open fire and the body heat of many customers. England's smallest inn is the Smith's Arms at Godmanstone, Dorset, with a seating capacity of only 28. In the fifteenth century it was a working blacksmith's forge

The Decoyman's Cottage, Abbotsbury Swannery, Dorset.

In 1824 much of this thatched cottage was destroyed in the 'Great Storm'

and remained so until, it is said, King Charles II, who became King in 1660, stopped to have his horse shod and asked the smith for a drink. On finding there was no licence to sell drink from the forge the King granted him one on the spot. The use of thatch, even when a high-risk occupation is carried out in the building, shows it can be as safe as any other roofing material, for many thatched forges still exist.

Regional variations in thatching styles were once more common than they are today. No railways, few roads, little education and low incomes all helped to keep particular methods strong within their locality. Although the thatcher may mark his work today with an individual roof finial, ridge peak or elaborate ridge pattern, his style used to be dictated by regional factors. Variations in technique were most common in coastal regions, mountainous areas, offshore islands, Scotland, Wales and Ireland, where it often proved necessary to secure the thatch with more than just extra spars. Many of these areas have lost their traditional ways in the last hundred years and vernacular styles are kept alive only by rural life museums.

On Skye, off the west coast of Scotland, there are three museums founded on old crofters' thatched cottages to show what life was like there until fairly recently. At Colbost a black-house depicts life there a hundred years ago and a crofter's house is preserved at Luib. In Kilmuir a group of thatched buildings at the Skye Museum of Island Life are kept in good repair by the only thatcher in the area, Jonathan MacDonald.

Onshore gales and turbulent squalls could easily lift corners of thatch, and just as slates and roof tiles can be ripped from the roof once the wind has gained a small entry point so the same can happen with thatch. The roof covering was secured by a variety of means: a series of ropes crisscrossing the roof was one method, or sometimes

discarded fishing nets were used. The rope method, chosen by most thatchers on the Isle of Man, had a twofold purpose – to hold the thatch on the roof for a short period of time and then to release it to mulch the ground. Although the Isle of Man is small, there too there were regional variations.

The thatch of the Manx Croft was described by Blundell in 1657. He wrote, 'Their habitations are mere hovels compacted with stone and clay for the walls, thatched with broom.' Little change had taken place by 1725 when a visitor named Waldron recorded 'the houses of the peasantry are no more than cabins made of sods and covered with the same except for a few of the better kind thatched with straw'.[8]

At Cregneash, a village in the shadow of the Meayall Hill, overlooking the Calf of Man, straw thatch was favoured. In other areas ling, marram grass or rushes could often be seen fixed to the 'scraa' – sods of grass – applied with the earth side downwards on planks laid over the rafters.

Cregneash was one of the last strongholds of the traditional skills and customs which characterized the crofter's way of life. 'Harry Kelly's Cottage' was built in the early eighteenth century and today is preserved as part of the Cregneash Folk Museum where the largest area of thatch on the island can now be found. The Museum now fears that Cregneash will become the only place on the Isle of Man where thatched roofs are to be seen, and this only with the assistance of a local farmer who grows a suitable straw for the purpose. The cottage, which was once the home of the typical fluent Manx speaking fisherman-crofter who also quarried slates is, not surprisingly, built of rough slate walls that are two feet (0.6 metres) thick and firmly set in mortar. The straw was heaped on top of the 'scraa' and then held in place not by hazel spars but by a series of twisted straw ropes called 'suggane' which were then secured to the stones that protruded from the top of the

Harry Kelly's cottage at Cregneash, Isle of Man.

This cottage retains its traditional thatch thanks to the Manx Museum and a local farmer

cottage walls. These were known as 'bwhid suggane' and proved useful to hang herrings on to dry. Sometimes briars were woven into the straw rope for extra strength. Thatched dwellings such as these were once common but today their ruined walls can be seen scattered over the surrounding countryside.

An account rendered in 1803 for a cottage constructed at Close y Kee on the Isle of Man amounted to £43 11s 10d. Out of this sum '£2 12s 6d was paid to Pat Quirk for thatching the house, 2s 10d for lath and nails, 7s fill beaming the house and getting up scraas, briars for thatching the house 10s, 4 doz. thatch 14s'.[9] and probably differed little in cost from half a century before.

The islanders in the north favoured a local marram grass, which they called 'bent', found growing along the sandy coast from Kirk Michael to the Point of Ayre. 'Bent' did not grow and was rarely used in the south; instead, they might use: wheat, oat or barley straw, reeds grown in the north, two types of rush, ling or broom. In 1988 marram grass was removed from a cottage roof in the north of the island and replaced by a longer-lasting coat of Norfolk reed by Master Thatcher Peter Brugge who had travelled from the mainland to undertake the work.

Not all offshore islands secured their thatch with ropes or nets. The Isle of Wight favoured a conventional wheat-straw thatch and today most buildings have been re-coated in combed wheat reed, with much of it ferried to the island by hauliers.

A change of material on an old roof can still lead to a tasteful appearance. Today, a combed wheat-reed thatch applied in the long-straw style with traditional eaves sparring enhances the 300-year-old former post office at Witchampton, Dorset. Once part of the Crichel Estate it shows three stages in house development before reaching its existing shape. In 1989 it was thatched by Tony Cottrell of Wimborne, who used 8,000 spars not only for the decorative patterns but for fixing the new thatch to the old coatwork. Close by is what is claimed to be the longest stretch of thatch over domestic properties. However, the 120 yards (110 metres) of thatch covering 11 cottages now shows a variety of materials and thatching styles.

Leprosy was prevalent in all parts of Europe until the fourteenth and fifteenth centuries, which led to many towns building leper hospitals on their outskirts. Thatch proved the most suitable roofing material although there may have been a certain reluctance on the part of the thatcher to maintain the roof. The thatched roof was easy to construct and could be fumigated

The Old Post Office, Witchampton, Dorset.
Over 8,000 spars were used here by thatcher Tony Cottrell in 1989. Combed wheat reed has been applied in the long-straw style

St Margaret's, Taunton, Somerset.

This long stretch of plain thatch cannot claim to be ornate but suits the style of St Margaret's, once the site of a leper hospital

with smoke if necessary and easily demolished. St Margaret's, Taunton was a leper hospital until cases decreased, and in the sixteenth century was rebuilt as almshouses. Appropriately for a building that has survived from the early days of thatch it now houses the Guild of Somerset Craftsmen as well as the Rural Development Commissions's Thatching Officer for the South-West.

The arrival of the Agricultural Revolution worried the labourer far more than the thatcher, for he could see the disappearance of his wet-weather threshing work and a reduction in the number of farm workers. The thatcher probably bemoaned the quality of his working material as produced by the new machines but it must have been many years before he saw a real threat to his livelihood. By 1787 change had swept across the country, and although at first it had

been more noticeable in the new industrial areas and the larger farms of the north where experimental techniques were readily adopted, new ways were soon to encroach upon even the most rural areas. New tools and machinery led to the construction of new buildings to house them in and few of these were thatched. The new consolidated areas of enclosed land led to the construction of new farmhouses at a central point. A preference for the substantial square design saw a depth of building quite unsuitable for the steeply sloped pitch required by the thatched roof. Neither did the new layout for the farmyard include a design for the traditional threshing floor. Instead, a horse-engine house was added and inside the barn stood a new machine. The threshing machine had arrived and with it the first real threat to the thatcher's materials.

2

The thatcher's thatch

Today the thatcher may apply his thatch to the roof by traditional means or he may decide to use the latest materials. Steel rods and metals crooks can replace hazel sways, liggers and spars, and the thatcher may even tease his material into place with an aluminium beadle, or leggett, while resting on an aluminium extension ladder. He has found ways to overcome many of the problems he has had to face and has sometimes had new tools made. Some thatchers improvise by making their own wooden leggetts, knee pads and palm straps, and tour car boot sales in search of suitable hooks but the greatest crisis in recent years has not been so easy to solve. There has been an inadequate supply of thatching materials to satisfy present demands.

The thatching industry is very buoyant at the moment and this has led to difficulties in some areas in maintaining a steady supply of thatch for the craftsmen. The 1990s will be a decade of research into ways of overcoming many of the problems that have hit the supply of traditional British thatching materials. Just as interest in the maintenance of the underwood waned and economics dictated hazel should be replaced by conifers, which led to a shortage of spars,

so farmers ceased growing long-stemmed varieties of wheat that were prone to gale damage, especially in fields that had had their hedges removed. They favoured short-stemmed crops that yielded more grain but no thatching reed. No longer was it of prime importance to maintain their own supply of thatching reed as there were often no thatched buildings left on the farm and no ricks.

It was not just the combed wheat-reed thatchers and the long-straw thatchers who were encountering problems with their materials. Water reed (*phragmites australis*) had once been the vernacular roofing material of the areas in which it grew. Along river estuaries, some coastal waters such as Abbotsbury, Weymouth and Arne, the Fens and, best known of all, the Norfolk Broads, beds of water reed grew in abundance. Much of the 'Norfolk reed' is now not grown in Norfolk at all but in the big thatching counties of Suffolk, Essex and Cambridgeshire. In Norfolk the reed beds are in decline.

Carefully managed reed beds can produce long, straight-stemmed reeds that would last the best part of a lifetime in favourable conditions. Reed grows best in managed beds where rhizomes can descend as many feet into the soft alluvial soil as the reed towers above ground level, and best results are obtained by keeping the bed clear of weeds and undergrowth that will quickly invade. The rhizome likes to be treated to a programme of water lapping around the base of the stems alternating with a dry period. Too much or too little water can affect the crop just as lack of cutting, pollution, pleasure craft, erosion, accumulating silt and cutting restrictions imposed by nature reserves have all taken their toll of the great British reed beds. Today the problems of the reed beds are being investigated by the University of East Anglia, deterioration of thatch by Bath University and maintaining supplies and use of thatch by the Rural Development Commission, the National Council for Master Thatchers and the Thatching Advisory Service.

Annual cutting, known as Single Wale, is favoured at Abbotsbury where commercial reed beds cover 50 acres of land adjacent to the Swannery reserve. Reed provides an anchorage for the soil in the water-washed beds, stabilizing the surface. Rhizomes spread their root systems like 'a mat of giant spaghetti', as one reed-cutter described it in

Triticale thatching reed grown in Dorset.

Triticale, a hybrid wheat mother crossed with a rye father, is a recent addition to the thatcher's reed source

Abbotsbury reed beds, Dorset.

Reed-cutter Tony 'Dick' Dalley (*second left*) recalled that one year the last load of Abbotsbury reed was pulled from the reed bed with water lapping at the axles of the trailer

1990. Even where the commercial crop is grown, care is taken to establish a balanced environment and screens of reed are left at the perimeter of the beds.

When supplies of British reed could not keep pace with the demand, enterprising suppliers turned an eye to the Continent where vast tracts of suitable land are managed to produce a commercial reed crop. Countries were quick to realize the potential of the British market. Devon reed importer Peter Grimley favours Dutch reed and regularly plies the route from the edge of Dartmoor to Dover wih his 60-foot (18-

metre) long lorries and trailers. After crossing the Channel by ferry he collects his reed from a variety of sources. He has watched Dutch water reed being cut with large mechanical machines on caterpillar tracks while standing on the frozen lakeside. Huge ricks of reed stretch as far as the eye can see, showing the potential of reed beds where sufficient interest is shown in commercial production. Both large and small farming enterprises take part and the Grimley lorry with its personalized number plate of 'TDV' (Thatchers' Delivery Vehicle) can be found alongside an elderly

Thatcher Stephen Pope working at Melbury Osmond, Dorset.

Imported reed can be thick-stemmed and coarse like this Turkish reed. Stephen Pope regretted leaving his protective knee-pads at home

Fordson tractor pulling a small trailer-load of reed or a large stack. Back in Devon the reed is unloaded into large barn-like stores until it is required by thatchers from all over the country. Small loads are often collected by local thatchers or large quantities are loaded into a lorry by a barn conveyor belt and delivered direct to the site. Combed wheat 'Devon' reed as it is locally known (because it was in that county that a reed comber was invented) is not as common today and Devon is now a county of mixed materials and thatching styles. It is possible to see Devon long houses being restored with a new thatch of Dutch reed.

Not all imported reed comes from Holland or is harvested in the same way. French reed from the Camargue, water reed from Poland and Turkey, to mention but a few sources, have found their way to the great British thatching counties. Alan Grey-Hodder left the Royal Navy for a more peaceful life thatching in the Dorset countryside and often uses imported Turkish reed as well as the local 'spear' reed grown at Abbotsbury.

Turkish reed grows to such a length that bunches are often trimmed to fit the shipping containers that bring it to Britain. The shaggy flower-head is intact showing that the country of origin does not suffer from severe frosts near the reed beds. Machines for cutting the reed were exported to Turkey in the hopes that they could replace the labour-intensive method of harvesting with hooks but the scheme did not work. The men would not adapt to mechanized cutting and the machines were rendered useless within a season.

The quest for new materials led to the invention of plastic thatch which was greeted with a mixed reception. Hailed by some as the salvation of the thatcher's craft and scorned by others as a cheap imitation that would not fool anyone, its production was shortlived. In 1972 it was announced in the press 'The Twentieth Century has finally caught up with the last of the great British crafts – thatching.' It was claimed that plastic thatch would 'bring the picture postcard look back to villages throughout the country. It was claimed to be bird-proof, fire-proof and watertight and looked like 'best Norfolk reed'.

Norfolk thatcher Bob Farman, in the same article, disagreed: 'I have seen this stuff and I suppose if you have not got very good eyesight and stand far enough away it could pass for thatch – It will never replace traditional thatch'. The columnist remarked 'How will it be sold, I wonder? Custom-tailored – shaped like a tea cosy and a guaranteed fit by return of post? or Stretch thatch – your old home like new in minutes – to cover any and every cottage?'

The article also quoted a Wiltshire thatcher, Mr Albert Maggs, who thought 'it might just catch on. It could bring new life to the industry'.[1] However this was not to be for there were problems. Plastic thatch arrived by the roll and it was claimed it could be fixed by anyone. Some applied it direct to the existing thatch and this method did help cushion the noise and retain some insulation, but others applied it to felt and battens. The sound of torrential rain was deafening and one inhabitant described it 'as being as noisy as living under galvanised iron sheeting'. Plastic thatch had none of the properties of real thatch that kept the house warm in winter and cool in summer. Other problems quickly arose: subjected to summer heat and winter cold joints began to prise apart and roofs to leak. One cottage owner who had given in and replaced his traditional combed wheat-reed thatch on his period cottage with plastic thatch found his roof leaked in this way. As the firm was no longer operating he could not obtain fresh supplies and had to resort to sealing the cracks with an adhesive gun. While he toiled on the house roof two thatchers calmly ridged his thatched garage with combed wheat reed encountering no problems at all.

Plastic thatch at Godmanstone, Dorset, 1990.

A modern thatching material that was supposed to solve the thatchers' supply problems

Sadly, today the period cottage has a roof of tiles with the local authorities not insisting a traditional thatched coat should be restored; its character has been totally destroyed.

Other thatching materials have met with problems too. Rushes once grew in profusion around every farm pond and some villages had as many as 27 such ponds so the quantities available were really useful. They were harvested green by the thatchers to thatch the farm ricks. When cattle troughs and piped water replaced the need for pond water for animals, and cart wheels no longer needed periodic soaking to tighten the bond between rim and felloes, the ponds disappeared with little regard to the value of rushes or wildlife. Oat straw was replaced by longer-lasting materials, and heather, which had for a short while enjoyed popularity amongst the landed gentry, fell from favour and sheep browsing on moors and heaths nibbled the young growth.

On the Isle of Skye, where most men knew traditional thatching methods earlier this century, few thatch today. One thatcher is Jonathan MacDonald who lives at Duntulm and keeps the practice alive at Kilmuir using common rush. However, just as thatching methods have evolved all over the country so today he uses wire mesh

Thatcher Jonathan MacDonald at work on the Isle of Skye.

Rush is still used in the 1990s at the Museum of Island Life on the Isle of Skye, where Jonathan MacDonald believes in preserving the traditional ways of island life

rather than heather bonds to keep the rush in place. No spars are needed for this method of thatching. Few houses are thatched today on Skye, where the population that peaked at 21,000 in 1821, declined to 15,000 60 years later and has now dropped to under 9,000, with most people employed in agriculture and tourism.[2]

Once heather thatch was valued by heath dwellers, Welsh upland farmers and Scottish crofters, where it was secured by ropes called 'sugans' or 'siomans' on vernacular buildings, and everywhere it produced a long-lasting roofing material. Thatcher William Tegetmeier of York has found a plentiful source of suitable material, courtesy of the National Trust, and hopes to be able to thatch his first roof in heather in

1990. At least two thatchers are currently using heather: in Kent one thatcher harvests his heather on the Weald and John Warner from Warwickshire has to date thatched a farmhouse near Bardon Mill, Northumberland and a barn near Grassington in heather.

Many roofs of heather in the New Forest area are nearing the time when they will need re-thatching but it is unlikely that many owners will appreciate heather enough to seek a replacement coat, and in the area of Wareham Heath other roofing materials have already replaced the heather that was once so popular and freely available.

The thatcher seeks the long-stemmed heather called 'Ling' that grows taller than the garden variety and is cut and baled in long lengths. He trims the bales to length and fixes the heather to the roof complete with the flower-head and bushy upper branches and as it ages it takes on a warm black hue. Popular from the 1880s until the First World War and extolled by organizations such as the Country Gentleman's Association, expensive transport costs and a lack of appreciation has led to a decline in the number of buildings thatched with what was considered the most beautiful and long-lasting thatching material of all. Perhaps the goodwill found by William Tegetmeier could be extended to other areas.

Heather had many other uses. Fine brooms were made at Verwood, Dorset and Winlaton, Durham; heather formed the base for roads across marshy ground, and in the south heather was mixed with clay for cob walls and heather mattresses were prized. The root also had its uses for pegs, nails, hooks and spars.

Today, water reed is the only naturally grown thatch that is well used but the British Reed Growers Association sadly draws attention to a general decline. In some counties conservation areas include what were once productive reed beds.

Neglected reed beds rapidly revert to unusable distorted reed if regular harvesting is not carried out. Unfortunately, the importance of British reed is not brought to the notice of many country lovers and they are not prepared to allow cutting even on a rotation basis. However, in some areas the ideal solution seems to have been found. At Abbotsbury, Dorset, where a wide variety of wildlife, besides the renowned swan colony, benefits from a protected habitat, reed management is practised with wildlife in mind. Adjacent to the Swannery a commercial crop of reed is grown.

Swans, ducks and one stray flamingo form the top of the food chain at the Swannery where they benefit from their organic (i.e. natural – unpolluted and untreated) surroundings. Smaller creatures can be seen by the patient observer, from hides screened by mats of harvested reed. Reed buntings, marsh, reed and sedge warblers can be seen in reed beds throughout the country. The bearded tit is rarely seen away from beds of phragmites reeds and neither is the marsh harrier. Old reed is necessary to encourage reed and sedge warblers to weave their delicate cup-shaped nests. There

Abbotsbury Swannery, Dorset.

Reed benefits both wildlife and man at Abbotsbury. A commercial reed bed lies next to the Swannery where reed forms a valuable wildlife habitat

Abbotsbury reed beds, Dorset. Reed-cutter 'Dick' Dalley supervises the harvest.

The rhizomes grow as many feet deep as the water reed grows high. A converted Allen scythe is used to harvest the crop between January and April

would be disastrous results if attempts were made to weave a nest on young slippery stems!

An air of tranquillity rests over the commercial reed beds for most of the year and wildlife here is hardly disturbed by the small amount of maintenance required to clear ditches. Even when the reed is cut soon after Christmas, when the high tides have passed and the water level has dropped and frost has shrivelled much of the outer leaf and flower-heads, a screening belt of standing reed is left close to the boundary fence for wildlife. Voles and other small rodents soon take up residence in such areas and in turn are preyed upon by short-eared owls, harriers and other birds of prey. In Norfolk reed beds the swallowtail butterfly

is encouraged to breed by the presence of milk parsley growing in the organic beds.

Cutting is no longer carried out by hand but neither has it reached a highly mechanized point that could be detrimental to the careful balance that is maintained. Undisturbed by the conversation amongst the reed cutters and the purr of the converted Allen scythe that is propelled through the reed beds to harvest the crop, a hawk hovered overhead, living testimony to the harmony that can be achieved. Reed-cutter Tony 'Dick' Dalley guides the reed towards the machine which is propelled through the crop, cutting a small swathe at a time. Not all of his 28 seasons have been spent cutting the reed by machine. He recalls his first years when he cut in a gang of eight using special hooks, under the guidance of Willie Limm, who still lives in the village and learnt his skills from the Swanherd who was known affectionately by his staff as 'Uncle Joe' Gill. The gang adopted a staggered formation to avoid cutting each other as they cut a swathe.

The early gales of 1990 caused extensive damage in the area that had virtually escaped damage during the 1987 hurricane. Large areas of reed lay flattened just before harvesting was due to start and, besides reducing the crop, harvesting became more difficult. Little damaged reed can be retrieved for thatching and most has to be burnt on site. The practised eye of the reed-cutter predicts a crop of some 700 bundles from this bed, that yielded 1,000 the previous year. However, what does remain standing is of a high quality and stands tall and straight, without bent necks, just as the thatcher hopes to see it.

Various machines have been tried; the Allen scythe has proved most satisfactory but spare parts are becoming increasingly difficult to find. The British Reed Growers Association purchased a larger machine but it proved useless on the small Norfolk reed beds that are surrounded by dykes, and had to be sold. On the Fens a converted rice cutter was in use in 1984 but more mechanized methods are being used on large acres of reed beds. Experiments are still continuing and Dorset thatcher Alan Grey-Hodder is trying to perfect a technique using a larger machine with balloon tyres which he hopes will counteract the extra weight and prevent the machine from sinking into the soft soil.

Cleaning the reed is a much more pleasant job than flailing the wheat and removing the chaff must have been. The cleaned stems are placed in an improvised measure, straightened and then tied with plastic twine. When 'Dick' Dalley learnt to cut the reed by hand he wove a bond of willow to tie each bundle and even today favours this method. Continental reed is often tied by flat plastic bonds or even with wire, which means the thatcher has to carry wire cutters with him on to the roof to open the bundles.

Butting each bundle produces a tidy tight reed with even ends that will stand shifting and stacking until it is required by the thatcher. The final job of the day is burning the debris left from the cleaning process and

Abbotsbury reed beds, Dorset.

Clean reed pleases the thatcher. The shrivelled leaf and any broken stems are allowed to fall from the bunch

Abbotsbury reed beds, Dorset.

Butting the ends on the ground produces a neat bundle though care must be taken when handling the reed as untreated cuts turn septic within 24 hours

any flattened reed to leave the bed clean for the next year's growth. All operations are completed before the new vigorous green shoots burst through the surface.

The stiff stems of marsh reed will not make a satisfactory ridge and for this purpose sedge, rush or wheat straw is used. Sedge grows in the same areas as marsh reed and is often encouraged as a complementary crop. It is harvested green at any time of the year, on a four-year rotation, when sufficient growth has been made.

Peter Brugge of Master Thatchers North, who lives in Cheshire but works in Scotland, has thatched around the areas of Hawick and Rhu, but when he thatched in

Fortingall, near Loch Tay, he found the vernacular ridge was concrete and this was the style he replaced.

Wheat thatch differs from water reed in several ways although its water shedding abilities are the same. The methods of harvesting have progressed from the days when reaping hooks or scythes laid the crops for women to gather into sheaves that were bound with straw ropes. Children 'wimbling' hay bonds were a common sight last century.

Progress cannot always improve the harvest for the thatcher. Combine harvesters chop the stems of wheat reed into unusable stubble and a reaper and binder must still be used today if thatching reed is required.

North Poorton Manor House, Dorset.

Water reed is not pliable and sedge is often used for ridging, as is the case here, where thatcher Guy Gale is seen assisted by S.M. Gay

A field at Leigh, Dorset.

Reaper-binders have been brought out of retirement and are now earning their keep as valuable working machines once more

Unfortunately, by the time it was realized that these time-honoured machines would still be needed, many had already been scrapped. Reaping the wheat crop is definitely more successful when the old combination of a low-powered tractor of the same vintage is used to pull the machine. Compatibility between the old reaper and a new powerful tractor cannot be achieved and problems arise that cause frequent delays.

Ricks of thatching reed used to be seen in fields, rick bartons and also in forage yards, for any sheaf of long-stemmed wheat could

be used after threshing had removed the grain. The Willis forage yard stood close to Sherborne town station and filled with ricks as the harvest progressed, ensuring an adequate supply of thatching materials, after a good harvest, to last for much of the year. Up to 16 corn ricks could be fitted into the yard as well as several hay ricks. More ricks filled the rick barton at the Lime Kiln Farm half a mile away. The thatcher who thatched their ricks would return at a later date to purchase some reed. Mr Wilfrid Willis recalls his family would often be eating breakfast when the same thatcher would arrive in the hope of purchasing a good quality reed. In years of bad harvests inferior reed often had to be purchased to try to maintain supplies. Large quantities purchased by Willis's from the harvest field would sometimes be delivered direct to the thatcher's home. At first this was by wagon and horses, later by a Sentinel steam lorry and then by a Ford 25 cwt. lorry with a brass radiator. The lorry extended the working area as far as Cornwall. Horses were still used for local deliveries and 12 were usually kept at the forage-yard stables, sometimes as many as 20. Their wagons

delivered a ton of reed at a time. Today a lorry can deliver six tonnes.

In November 1958 the thatcher rendered his account for work completed at Lime Kiln rick barton as follows:

1 Reed Rick	1	5	0
4 Hay Ricks	6	15	0
8 Corn Ricks	10	10	0
600 Long Spars at 9/-	2	14	0
Total cost of Thatching	£21	4s	0d[3]

The fear generated by the introduction of new methods and machines amongst the

A field at Yetminster, Dorset.

The two small ricks of Aquila wheat sheaves will stand beneath tarpaulins. Although they will not be thatched, the fact that they were built at all in 1988 indicates the change of feeling towards thatch

agricultural labourers accelerated after the introduction and acceptance of the threshing machine. As early as 1789, only two years after the first practical design for a threshing machine was demonstrated, incidents demonstrating this fear were reported in the south of England, far away from Scotland and the northern counties where most of the machines could be found.

Early Sunday morning three ricks were discovered to be on fire, at a very considerable distance from each other, near the town of Chard, which were entirely burned or rendered useless. They must have been purposely set on fire and it is earnestly to be wished that the infamous wretches who were the cause of it may be discovered, and brought to condign [fitting] punishment.[4]

The smashing of machinery was soon to follow. By December 1830 groups of rioters could be found all over the country:

On the evening of Wednesday last, a messenger arrived in Sherborne from Milborne Port, bringing information that a body of rioters had assembled during the day, and had caused a thrashing machine belonging to Mr Grey of Henstridge to be burnt. They then proceeded to Yenstone, and destroyed a machine of Mr Davis, and from thence to Tomer Farm, where they burnt two machines.[5]

An article published in 1861 by the Bath and West Society in its Journal listed the main developments in agriculture during the previous 20 years. Mr Morton said the mobile threshing machine had been introduced in 1841 and in his view there was 'no class of machines of which the usefulness and economy have so rapidly commended themselves to farmers generally', adding that Messrs Clayton of Lincoln were sending out ten machines weekly.

Threshing was traditionally winter work whether by flail, a hand- or horse-powered threshing machine installed in a barn, or by mobile threshing tackle in the barton

or field and so it is today. Attitudes have changed since the introduction of the threshing machine and today the whole process is of novelty value and attracts a crowd of spectators.

Winter threshing weather is often unpredictable and the biting wind often drives the waste chaff into the operators' faces, but it is essential to thresh the opened rick as quickly as possible. If just a threshing machine is used the stems of the wheat will usually be delivered in an unsorted pile and this becomes long-straw thatch. The thatch puller was the man who pulled handfuls from the long-straw rick which had been made after the threshing machine had finished its work. The handfuls grew into bundles that were bound with straw bonds and gradually enough bundles were drawn to supply the thatcher for the following day's work. In 1953 Anthony Pearman found a thatch puller at work in the spring:

Two ricks of recently thrashed wheat-straw lie with a space of about ten paces between them. A bitterly cold east wind was driving right between the ricks. So, as the bundles were completed they were placed to windward, and built up so that in a few hours they formed a head-high breastwork from one to the other, in the lew [lee] of which he worked for several days[6]

until the rick had been turned into neat bundles of long-straw thatch. The ingenuity of the countryman usually found a way of making life more comfortable when working in the open air. The hedger would light a fire from his hedge trimmings close to where he was working to warm himself by but there was little the thatcher could do, except start work on the best aspect of the house in winter.

One of the earliest bills for thatching to survive, as opposed to a ledger, was written in 1771 by Edward Freke, a literate thatcher, who had completed some work for a Mr Fricker

Threshing at Yetminster, Dorset.

Threshing today is still winter work. The biting wind drives clouds of dust and chaff into the operators' faces

for straw	1	10	0
for making of thatch		3	0
for 4 days work thatching and labour		8	0
for spars and tarline, laths and nails		4	2
	£2	5s	2d[7]

Edward Freke made his thatch by pulling his own straw from the rick. He also mentioned using tarline (an unusual name for tarred cord) at this early date. Before tarred cord was available the thatcher used honeysuckle stems or blackberry brambles to tie his base coat of thatch to the roof timbers. The reed puller used to be paid a penny a bundle but it was bemoaned in 1935 that wages had increased by five and thatching straw had not increased in price.

One expert hedge layer of Briantspuddle with a long family history of farm work recalled how he and his sister pulled the thatch for their father who thatched the farm ricks. He would meet them at the school bus stop in the afternoon carrying their old clothes and they would work for as

47

long as it took to pull enough bundles of long-straw thatch for the next day's ricks. The children had to place the bundles in a circle around the rick and not in a pile so that the thatcher would not have to walk too far. On occasions they would be required to hand the bundles up to their father on the rick and would work on during the long summer evenings and into the night, sometimes until three o'clock in the morning. There was not much sleep before it was time to get up to catch the school bus again.

Thatchers in Norfolk and Bedfordshire where long-straw roofs still exist in large numbers, outnumbering the roofs in Norfolk reed that many people expect to predominate, refused to let their vernacular style die out when long straw became in short supply. Some solved this problem by growing their own thatching materials.

Not everyone favoured long-straw thatch and ways were sought to adapt the threshing machine to thresh only the ears of grain. In many areas reed had been combed by drawing it from a large wooden press assembled in a barn to clean it and often the ears were removed with an old scythe blade mounted in a wooden stand. In Somerset in 1808 the reed was drawn through an iron-toothed comb but soon experiments were taking place in Devon to produce a reed comber to fit on top of the standard threshing machine. The sheaves were opened and fed into the comber which presented only the ears to the threshing drum. The undamaged but clean stems then passed through the machine to emerge in an orderly manner to the tyer. The tyer, a device at the rear of the threshing machine, measured the bundle, automatically tied it and ejected it onto the ground. The bundles are then butted on to a spot-board on the ground to even the ends. The few remaining long ends are then trimmed with a pair of shears. In the past this was a job that was usually left for the thatcher to do himself.

Reed combers that have been in use for over 100 years suffer from wear and many are no longer as efficient as they once were. It has become impossible to find a machine in good working condition at a reasonable price. They do not always completely empty the ear of grain and sometimes fresh green shoots appear on a newly thatched roof, especially on the ridge, where the grain in the ears lies close to the surface. Ways to overcome this problem have been investigated in recent years. Plans for building a new reed comber were drawn up in 1976 by the Rural Development Commission (formerly CoSira) following the original 'Murch' design and six machines have been built by thatchers in their spare time. The first machine to be built by an engineer as a commercial project was completed in 1988 by agricultural engineer Edwin Parrott, for a Dorset farmer. The difference between this machine and the old reed combers is that the frame is built of welded steelwork instead of wood but the belt, conveyors and combing drums are identical to the original machines. The project was found to be an interesting challenge as Edwin Parrott knew nothing whatsoever about the machine, but now that he understands its workings and has seen the finished product in action he feels there are improvements that could be made to suit modern methods and make it more efficient. However, the original project was time consuming rather than difficult in engineering terms and pressure of work has prevented him from implementing his plans to date.

At Chield-Mearc Farm, Wiltshire, Stuart Hayward, who in 1989 grew 60 acres of Aquila wheat thatching reed and 20 acres of Maris Widgeon, has invented a mobile reed comber. He has been growing reed for thatching from winter-sown varieties for 20 years since giving up dairy farming. Although his family have not thatched themselves he has close connections with the

Threshing at Yetminster, Dorset.

Combed wheat reed descends to the tyer, a machine that carefully measures and ties a bundle. All that remains then is for the bundles to be butted on a spot-board to even the ends

Threshing at Yetminster, Dorset.

Uneven lengths may be trimmed with a pair of shears. The thatchers often tidied the ends themselves

craft for his father used to produce and 'draw' long-straw thatch. The mobile comber can cut and thrash between three and five acres a day, depending on the weather and the density of the crop and can produce in the region of 1,000 bundles daily. The machine took him six years to develop, and is similar to the Murch pattern, from a 1951 B 64 International trailer combine with the cutter mechanism removed and a 1940 vintage binder. The machine works well in ideal conditions when the crop is at exactly the right stage of ripeness. Before using his own invention Stuart Hayward relied on a contractor from Fordingbridge in Hampshire to provide the threshing tackle. Most of the Chield-Mearc reed supplies thatchers in the Salisbury area of Wiltshire but one regular customer comes from Bognor Regis in West Sussex.

Farmer Michael Davies of Woodbridge Farm, Dorset grows about ten acres of thatching reed. After experimenting with Chalke Huntsman and Maris Widgeon he found the latter best, producing about 20 tons of thatching reed with a slightly lower grain yield than shorter-stemmed varieties grown as a grain crop.

Today Maris Widgeon, Maris Huntsman, Aquila and Triticale are favourite varieties for wheat thatching reed, replacing old favourites such as Little Joss, Elite, Square-headed Master, Red Standard and White Standard. In the Middle Ages less than one ton per two-and-a-half acres was the expected yield from their cereal crops. The crops were harvested by cutting off the ears and then gathering the thatching straw at a later date. Today the farmer expects yields in the region of seven tonnes by using the latest varieties.

Whatever thatching material is chosen it is bulky, and storage can be a problem. As the thatcher using British materials has to maintain a supply from one harvest to the next he often invests in a large quantity of reed if he has the capital and the storage space. The thatcher may not always be able to find any reed after a bad harvest, but if he has the storage space and can accept a large load direct from the farm, the straw merchant may give him preference when supplies are located.

Estate thatchers who rely on home produced materials will not have this problem; their materials will be supplied for them. After a good harvest 5,000 to 7,000 bundles of Abbotsbury marsh reed are stored in the tithe barn, proving sufficient for thatching estate cottages at Abbotsbury and Melbury Osmond. The surplus is sold to local thatchers. The reed has to be dry before it is stored in the barn as there is a high risk of spontaneous combustion from damp reed.

Thatchers with a long family involvement in the craft will often live on farms or smallholdings with sufficient storage space. Some loss may occur if the reed is stacked on the ground as damp will spoil the lower bundles and vermin may infest the rick. Some thatchers spread a layer of old reed on the ground to form a base for the reed stack. Perhaps the thatchers' love of cats and dogs stems partly from a wish to preserve their reed. Coypu that escaped from captivity caused extensive damage to beds of Norfolk reed until an extensive trapping programme reduced numbers. Today the British Reed Growers Association believes that the coypu may at last be extinct in these areas. The first coypu had escaped by 1932 and by 1960 numbers in the wild peaked at 200,000. Coypu fed on the rhizomes but to reach them they had to sever the reed, rendering the bed useless as the whole crop floated away. Coypu posed a threat to wildlife as well as to the thatcher, and trapping, at the height of the problem, was averaging a catch of 3,700 a month.

At Abbotsbury any damage is usually by the elements and the only culprit observed pecking grubs from the hollow stems of reed was a welcome visitor, a green woodpecker.

Abbotsbury tithe barn, Dorset.

This tithe barn still has agricultural connections as the cattle lorry shows. Abbotsbury reed is stored here until it is required by the thatcher

Thatching reed is delivered to Simon Garrett at Thornford, Dorset.

Thatchers today can find storage a problem. Three tonnes of Aquila combed wheat reed dwarfs the thatcher's truck that holds half a ton, a useful quantity to take with him each day

Near Bradford Abbas, Dorset.

Ron Gosney is seen here repairing his reed store, a disused cow byre, giving a new lease of life to a redundant farm building

Younger thatchers are often unable to store reed at their homes. Some have their materials delivered to the cottage they will be working on. A tarpaulin can cover a reed stack for a short period of time but once holes have been torn in it rain rapidly spoils the reed.

In the north of England there are fewer thatched houses than in the south but it is still important to maintain a steady supply of thatch. The problems of these northern thatchers differ from those of their southern counterparts for there are no materials locally available. Peter Brugge of Altrincham, Cheshire, relies on supplies of imported reed. House prices here are lower

53

Thatcher Peter Brugge at work in the Wirral.

Peter Brugge's working area is the north of England and sometimes Scotland, where no local reed is available. The ridge of this bungalow in the Wirral has been renewed with sedge and the distance the reed has to travel from the port may make thatchers question the viability of the craft. Spars have to be brought from as far away as Hampshire. However, Peter Brugge has undertaken new work for Balfour Beatty in Leicester and Derby who, like Fairclough Homes, see a future for the new thatched house in the north of England and if the current trend of popularity continues, hopefully there will be a future for these men; but in the meantime the thatchers pledge to continue, even in the most difficult circumstances.

The future of the thatcher's essential materials will rely heavily on the appreciation of the problems facing the craft by a wide spectrum of the population.

Encouragement from central government has been lacking to date and although farmers are encouraged to diversify from intensive methods they have not been tempted with proposals to explore the possibilities of growing marsh reed in suitable areas. The next ten years will show if there is a future for British thatching materials in quantities that can compete with imported reed but at the same time an appreciation of the value of the wood of the hazel and willow will also be needed. A regular supply of thatching materials will also require a steady supply of sparmaking wood that can only be supplied from carefully managed coppices.

3

The spar

The thatcher, the sparmaker and the farmer have been closely linked throughout history for they all had need of each other. It is questionable which came first, the management of hazel coppices or early attempts to thatch but both were required to make man's earliest shelter and have remained allied crafts. However, the thatcher's craft is appreciated by more people for he creates the finish that is visible on the roof and little thought is given to how his thatch is fixed in place. The number of spars on one cottage roof can exceed 5,000, so without the sparmaker the thatcher would find it difficult to function efficiently and good sparmakers are not easy to find.

Sparmaking is patient work that requires sitting in one position for long periods of time without loss of concentration. The woods favoured for spars today are hazel and willow, although some ash is used and one sparmaker experimented with the hard dogwood. In the past the young pliable suckers that grew from the base of elm trees were also cut for this purpose. The Anglo-Saxon word 'wych' means pliable and perfectly describes the twigs of the wych elm, or the Scots elm which is more numerous in the north of England where

hazel copses are few. Even though straight-grained woods are chosen the art of sparmaking is not easy and requires a definite knack, a straight eye and a razor-sharp spar hook. A slight lapse of concentration and the flesh can be cut to the bone.

Few thatchers make all of their spars today but those that do use a hook reserved for the purpose. Less than 50 years ago there was no shortage of materials or sparmakers and although large numbers of spars were needed by a thatching family, they knew how to obtain them and the suppliers were numerous. In some areas today there are no sparmakers left, few coppices and no young men showing an interest in taking up the craft. When a good sparmaker is found who can guarantee to supply thousands of spars at short notice, his name is passed on by word of mouth and he has no need to advertise. With improved communications and transport it is not unusual for the sparmaker to supply thatchers all over the country.

Many sparmakers are retired thatchers, hurdlemakers or disabled craftsmen who still have the use of their hands, but sparmaker Graeme Coombs took up the craft for the simple reason that he liked making spars. His father and grandfather had made spars but it was not their sole occupation, just as Graeme's son can make spars but prefers to thatch. Today the sparmaker's workshop is also his office, warmed by a woodburning stove that is fed the waste spar shavings and unsuitable spar gads. On the office wall is a distribution map with pins spaced as far apart as Essex, York, Wales, Kent, Cornwall and Oxford. An address book is always at hand and the telephone rings constantly. Graeme Coombs acknowledges the assistance of the Rural Development Commission, then CoSira, who helped get his enterprise started by backing his application for planning permission. They reasoned that he was situated in the heart of Dorset and could supply the county's thatchers. At this time no-one could have guessed his spars would be required from much further afield.

During the 1989 to 1990 season a million spars will have passed through Graeme Coombs' hands for the first time, of which he estimates he has made 250,000. Others

Sparmaker Graeme Coombs at work at King Stag, Dorset.
Graeme Coombs's sole occupation is making thatching spars – unusual in 1990

Sparmaker Graeme Coombs at King Stag, Dorset

The last bundle of 200 spars makes the number up to 20,000 and this load is bound for Oxford

are made for him by part-time sparmakers. Each year has seen an increase in demand that is expected to continue. One bundle of spars in his workshop is kept specifically to illustrate what the thatcher does *not* require; thick, uneven, knotted, badly pointed spars prove impossible to twist. The finely pointed triangles of hazel that fall from Graeme Coombs' gads are produced with a razor-sharp spar hook and are as regular in size as if produced by a machine, which as yet has proved impossible to invent.

The sparmaker's quest for wood takes him many miles from his workshop today.

At one time unproductive corners of fields and inaccessible slopes were put to good use as productive hazel coppices. The word 'coppicing' comes from the French word *couper*, meaning to cut, and until recently was thought to have been introduced by the Normans in the eleventh century.

Recent discoveries of Neolithic hurdles in the peat bogs of Somerset disprove this theory as they could only have been made by men who coppiced the underwood. Pollen analysis has shown that the hazel was one of the first trees to colonize after the ice retreated in about 7000 BC and was quickly

excellent pulley blocks and cog wheels but would not take a polish.

The hazel represented the largest crop of the underwood and the coppice often included standard trees such as oak. While the owner waited for his valuable oaks to mature he realized a smaller profit from the fast growing hazel. Not all coppices contained standards and the sparmaker and hurdlemaker preferred these for the gads grew tall and straight as they sought light through a thick canopy of leaves that formed a solid mat overhead. The woodsmen

Hazel coppice at Telegraph Hill, near Minterne Magna, Dorset.

This hazel coppice has not been cut for almost 40 years. To make it productive again action must be taken soon or the hazel will die

referred to the coppices as 'covers'. 'Covers' provided shelter belts for shooting parties too, but once estate owners cut down on both shooting parties and the management of their woodlands the hazel was one of the first to suffer, for it was not classified as woodland. However, before their decline early spring flowers thrived beneath the hazel and early catkins provided pollen for bees, autumn nuts filled the food stores of many woodland creatures and the hazel grew in such abundance from the Midlands to the south coast that many insects, including moths, green shieldbugs and nut-weevils thrived on hazel leaves.

Less thickly planted stools grew into bushes that were less productive. However, the declining interest in thatch and a fall in wool prices led to a slump in the demand for both sheep hurdles and spars and it was not long before landowners were seeking a more profitable timber crop. Grants encouraged farmers to plant large numbers of conifers, and although many small standings of hazel were left but neglected, larger coppices, often stretching for over 30 acres, were ripped out and in some areas landowners resorted to poisons, such as 245T (a herbicide), to kill the hazel. Wild flowers died with the hazel and wildlife moved elsewhere.

Today, highly productive hazel coppices fetch £100 an acre per year and those planted on rich damp soil mature in half the time of coppices with roots in barren slopes. Overgrown hazel coppices are cut back to the stools but little gad wood can be salvaged and is paid for by the bundle. A seven-year cycle can then be restored.

In 1876 Henry Conway, a general builder of Evershot, Dorset entered in his account book 'Paid 12/- per acre for Cutts Coppice'.[1] Post-war prices saw coppice at £3 per acre rising to £4 per acre in 1955. A leap to £20 to £30 per acre followed but then the price remained constant until increased demand led to the current rate. The sparmaker has to have an eye to the future, for his crop is cut in rotation and he needs sufficient acreage to enable him to set aside a maturing area ready for next year's harvest. Some coppices cannot be reclaimed economically for they are too small and inaccessible. Once, the sparmaker lived within a short distance of his coppice and relied on a donkey, horse and cart or quite often just his own two feet. Other coppices became cut off by the war effort when pastures were ploughed for the first time and cart tracks removed. A four-acre coppice on Thornford Hill was last cut in 1939 and is now getting past the stage when it could be reclaimed. After 40 years of neglect the hazel starts to die, but properly cut in strict rotation it can live for centuries producing over 20 useable gads from each stool.

One agricultural labourer who thatched the ricks on the farm where he worked rented a quarter of an acre of hazel coppice and found this sufficient for the spars he needed each year. This gave him an extra source of income and provided his family with small wood shavings that dried to make excellent lighting wood for his kitchen range.

Hazel gads are bundled ready to be removed from the coppice but today the smaller twigs are often burnt whereas once all of the wood was put to good use. Fine brush made faggot wood, which was always in demand for lighting kitchen fires before electricity reached rural areas. The finest twigs became sweet pea sticks and pea sticks that were counted into bundles of 25. Long rods made bean poles and sizable straight lengths became gads for spars or hurdles. Some rods were reserved for broom handles and any forked poles made useful clothes-line props. Very thin, long rods were saved to bind a newly laid hedge into position and others bound the layers of straw for bee skeps, baskets and at one time, straw furniture. Hoops were in demand to hold casks together for dry goods such as apples,

Coppice at Dyke Head plantation, Long Burton, Dorset.

Within weeks of being cut back to the stool fresh young growth emerges. In seven years time a useful crop of spar gads will be harvested

Hazel gads found at Whitfield Wood, Dorset.

These barley-sugar twists were caused by the honeysuckle vine and are prized by the walking-stick maker, but not the sparmaker who seeks straight gads

cheese, sugar, salt, fish and gunpowder, with the average worker making 400 hoops a day. Small forks were given to children for catapults and long pliable lengths made their long bows. The shepherd preferred to make his own crook from hazel to suit the neck size of his flock and the walking-stick maker was always looking for unusually shaped wood.

Although hazel can be cut after five years the gad will be smaller and fewer spars can be produced from it. Hurdlemaker Sidney Donald Davis considers early cutting can be detrimental to the long-term growth and prefers a minimum of seven years rotation.

Undergrowth and deer both take their toll of the crop. Deer are partial to most young green shoots and hazel is no exception although during a mild winter it may be spared. The only deterrent seems to be to clear a large portion of copse for deer do not like their habitat disturbed. Alternatively, stools can be protected with a layer of brushwood until the first growth is stronger. Deer are especially fond of ash shoots and will nibble at a clump until it is reduced to dust. The number of wild deer has increased in recent years. The noise of passing traffic can keep deer away but few coppices border a main road. Fencing the coppice is the only solution but it would be prohibitively expensive and deer can clear a surprising height.

It is not only deer that can make the hazel unusable for the sparmaker. It is important to keep the hazel stools clear of invasive climbing plants. Although the walking-stick maker may favour barleysugar twists when searching for suitable wood the thatcher does not. The strong climbing vine of the honeysuckle will distort the hazel and if left unchecked will ruin the whole stool. Other plants, like the strong vine of the giant bindweed, the thatcher's 'withywind', can produce a similar effect, withy being another name for a spar gad. However, before tarred twine was readily available the thatcher used strong vines such as these to tie his basecoat of thatch onto the rafters.

Spars can also be cut from the willow tree, whose shoots have the advantage of growing out of reach of browsing deer. There are 19 wild species of British willow, including the sallow and osier, but not all varieties can be made into spars and it is a question of trial and error. The thatcher can cut any willow into spar gad lengths but the wood will not always split into spars or twist into the hairpin shape required. One thatcher was given some gads cut from a tree he had not used before and none of it would make spars. If spar wood is in short supply the thatcher can use basket-makers' osiers that have not been cut for several years. Sparmaker Graeme Coombs has cut osiers on the Somerset Levels and they have made good spars.

Sources of willow can be harder to find although Rural Development Thatching Officer Paul Norman used mostly willow spars in Berkshire. It was once the tree that grew in damp areas adjacent to field ditches as well as along river banks. Mechanized cleaning of ditches led to many willows being felled to give access to the new machinery. The thatcher's saying was true:

> *That which grows in the wet*
> *Lasts longer in the wet.*

The willow spar outlives the hazel spar in the wet thatch.

Staunch Methodist and vergeside farmer Abel Moore valued his willow trees that bordered the River Wriggle in his field called Balsham. On discovering they had been inexpertly pollarded one night he was so incensed he made it the subject of his text at the chapel that Sunday:

> *Woe to the man that cut my withies down*
> *Balsham,*
> *And woe to the hook that cut them.*
> *He carried them home and cut them up small,*
> *And into the fire – consumed them all!*

Abel Moore had been counting on the mature willows producing his rick spars that

Thatcher Simon Garrett pollards a willow tree at Thornford, Dorset.

Pollarding is beneficial to the willow tree and reduces the weight of the limbs, that can split the trunk apart

Simon Garrett trims willow branches for spar gads at Thornford, Dorset.

The height of the pollarded willow is obvious, for the thatcher is standing in a ditch and the tree towers above him

year and could probably have forgiven the culprit more easily if the withies had been intended for spars but he could tell from the way they had been hacked from the stump that this was not their fate.

Willows grew in such profusion that Farmer Cooper at Wyke cut his on a four-year rotation and thatchers made between 20,000 and 30,000 rick spars annually for him and then thatched his ricks with rushes cut from around the farm ponds. Once the ricks had disappeared the willow was not as desirable, and not being suited to unlimited growth the excess weight of unpollarded limbs splits the trunks apart. Today the pollarding of willows is encouraged, as well as the management of hazel coppices. The Royal Society for Nature Conservation and Conservation Volunteers throughout the country have played their part in this operation which has centred on the trees of the Somerset Levels where willows grow in profusion. The willows have the ability to survive the five feet (1.5 metres) of water that lapped their trunks near Muchelney, Somerset during the floods of February 1990, but large hazel stools in exposed areas could not withstand the gale force winds that preceded the floods and many were uprooted and squashed flat on the ground, an event which does not appear to have happened before.

Working with hazel seems to suit everyone but some sparmakers complain of headaches every time they work with willow and this could be due to the constituent of aspirin it contains, which could also be the substance that deters woodworm beetles from boring holes in willow spars, although old hazel spars often crumble when removed from the roof because of the number of holes bored in them.

Whatever the wood used, the actual method of converting it into spars has remained unaltered for centuries. A cullodion print dating from about 1875 is an early and rare appreciation of the thatcher splitting his gad. The cullodion process was cheaper than its predecessor, the daguerreotype, but the price of six pence, complete with its small gilt frame, was beyond the pocket of most families. The larger cash payments made to the thatcher on completion of his work sometimes made it possible to indulge in luxuries such as these. At this time the use of the word spar was not universal and regional variations included spicks, spics, spears, specs,

Thatcher Simon William Garrett poses for a photograph at Over Compton, Dorset, *c.* 1868.

Sparmaking has not been mechanized. This collodion print shows the same method being used to split the gad over 100 years ago

Thatcher Simon Garrett, an expert sparmaker, at work at Thornford, Dorset.

Sharp points help the thatcher, who has to drive the spar into place on the roof

sprindles, pegs, pins, botches and broaches.

Spar hooks do wear with the constant need to keep them razor sharp using a grindstone. After many years and several handles the blade may become thin and unusable and sometimes it shows signs of metal fatigue after many years of stress caused by splitting the gad. Partially split spar gads make excellent holders for storing mature onions – a fact the thatcher made good use of.

Thinning the middle of the spar to make it easier to twist is commonly carried out by the thatcher who will use the finished product. Pressure of work today often makes it impossible for the full-time sparmaker to carry this out. It was possible to make 2,000 spars on a wet day and 70 years ago spars cost just ten shillings (50p) a thousand with many thatchers estimating to use this quantity each week.

Spars are sold to the thatcher in straight bundles today but until recent years they could be purchased twisted. Double twist is favoured by many thatchers, as they rightly claim the wood is lying at a more natural angle and so lasts longer. Single twisted spars used to be favoured by the thatchers of Somerset.

Many thatching families who had a large working area before the Second World War could not keep pace with the number of spars they required. Spars or spar gads were purchased in large numbers and many thatching families also rented their own coppice.

600 years after the Bishop's tenants cut spars for thatching, that probably included the Abbey roof at Sherborne, Dorset, the same productive coppice in Whitfield Wood was being rented by a thatcher. In the fourteenth century the Bishop's tenants paid their rent at the Michaelmas Hundred Court and it was their duty to carry four horse-loads of wood to Sherborne on each day the Bishop remained in residence. Each labourer was allowed one log per load for

Thatcher and sparmaker Simon Garrett, at work at Thornford, Dorset.

A quick hand and a keen eye are essential for the successful sparmaker

his own use and was paid 1½d a day. It was also their duty to gather gads for thatching purposes and each tenant received three spar gads per day for his services.[2] In 1960 the copse was poisoned and replaced by conifers.

Some thatchers obtained their gads from woodsmen. Charlie Davenport worked in Honeycomb and Almshouse Woods and sold spar gads but did not make spars. He also collected coal from the yard at Yetminster Station to deliver to the villagers of Thornford. In 1920 he took the day off for the house sale of the late General Clay, who had been the proud possessor of an outmoded form of transport – a brougham.

The body of the brougham was sold in one lot and converted into a cart but the leather hood was purchased by Charlie Davenport who took it off to spend the rest of its useful life as his shelter in the woods.

Some gads were delivered to the thatcher's yard and were then stored under apple trees and covered with a layer of thatch to stop them drying out in hot weather. Other gads were collected direct from the wood. Chris Childs could have been the subject used for the sparmaker John South in author Thomas Hardy's *The Woodlanders*, for Hardy regularly walked the circular route through Dogbury, High Stoy and the woods above Hermitage in Dorset where Chris Childs could be found. He carried his hurdles on his back in latter years but had once used a donkey. Spars were sometimes made in the outhouse of his cottage. When large numbers of gads were ready in the woods one year he hitched a ride with his nephew to one of the busiest thatching families in the area and was found sitting in their kitchen when they returned home from work. In this instance it was the thatcher's job to provide the transport and a lorry was hired which made two journeys to the wood.

When motor transport had replaced many of the horses some thatchers and sparmakers took advantage of the service that could be provided. The village of Hazelbury Bryan, not surprisingly, had its own sparmaker, Mr Granger, who worked the hazel coppices nearby and would have eight bundles of spars ready for the Thursday market bus. These would be placed on the luggage rack on the top of the bus with orders to leave them near Dancing Hill on the approach road to Sherborne. The 2,000 spars were placed behind railings by the conductor while the passengers waited patiently. On Friday this was repeated when the bus left for Yeovil market and another 2,000 spars were unloaded ready for the thatcher to collect much later in the day, and sometimes

Thatcher and sparmaker Simon Garrett, at work at Thornford, Dorset.

Whether a single-twist or double-twist spar is required the effort needed to twist it is apparent here

not until after dark. None were ever missing and none vandalized. It is unlikely such co-operation could be achieved today.

Demonstration roofs are a good way of showing people exactly how a thatched roof is constructed and a surprising number of spars are needed. Many thatchers demonstrate their skills at fêtes, fairs and agricultural shows but not many thatchers can equal the record of Harold Wright from the Somerset Levels who has demonstrated at the Royal Bath and West Show for 25

Harold Wright's demonstration roof at the Royal Bath and West Show, 1989.

The structure of the traditional thatched roof can be seen clearly on this demonstration model

Thatcher Stephen Pope's tools of his trade differ from those of the older master craftsmen. Work in progress at Melbury Osmond, Dorset.

Factory-made metal rods, crooks and tools are, in some areas, replacing the products of the underwood that were made by local craftsmen

years. Only a supple spar will twist easily so bundles of spars are soaked in water before they are required.

Less traditional methods can be seen in use today. On new work steel rods and metal hooks secure the thatch. Aluminium extending ladders are shorter and lighter to carry but colder to work on than wooden pole ladders. Tools are often difficult to obtain today and even in the early post-war years help was required from the Rural Industries Bureau to locate suppliers. At this time the Finch Foundry at Sticklepath, Devon still managed to supply essential hand tools but today some thatchers have resorted to having tools made for them. Aluminium beadles, or leggetts, have been cast for some thatchers; they appear not to wear but are cold to the hands. Just after the Second World War a few town smiths still existed and could be commissioned to make thatching hooks at a time when metal was in short supply.

Just as thatch is in vogue so the craft of the hurdlemaker is seeing a new lease of life. Sidney Donald Davis was born 70 years ago into what his father claimed was the largest family firm of hurdlemakers in this country,

Hurdlemaker Sidney Donald Davis of Milborne St Andrew, Dorset.

Sidney Donald Davis has a long history of hurdle- and sparmaking but nobody to carry on the family tradition

based at Milborne St Andrew, and completed a five year apprenticeship in his craft. The demand for hurdles slumped as the number of sheep kept by farmers dwindled. The family also made thatching spars, spent summer months hand-shearing sheep and previous generations gained certificates in turnip hoeing. Today Sidney Davis and his brother Montague work between six and eight acres of coppice a year on a seven- to eight-year rotation and make hurdles six feet (1.8 metres) long in heights of three, four, five or six feet (0.9, 1.2, 1.5 or 1.8 metres), charging £2.50 per foot (30 centimetres) height. The market is both local and further afield, as the number of hurdlemakers has dwindled and the Davis family knows of less than ten today.

Just after the First World War Wilf Moore made 12 sheep hurdles a day for Sherborne Castle Estate. He worked in an estate copse, cutting his own gads, and was paid one shilling for each hurdle he completed – a good wage at this time.

In March 1939 the Davis family account book shows: '5 dozen sheep hurdles at 23/- per dozen'. In December 1959 the price had risen to £10 per dozen. Today the popular

Traditional lambing pens at the Weald and Downland Open Air Museum, Sussex.

Sheep hurdles were once used in large numbers but lambing pens such as these are no longer a common sight

height for garden fencing is three or four feet (0.9 or 1.2 metres) and during the 1989 to 1990 season only eight sheep hurdles were made. For the annual Melplash show the regular order used to be for 40 dozen sheep hurdles each year measuring six feet by three feet (1.8 × 0.9 metres). For the 1990 show only ten dozen are required and for the Dorchester Show none at all, as iron hurdles are now used.

At one time last century the village of Winterborne Whitechurch could boast of 26 hurdlemakers, all of whom could make a living to satisfy the demand created by the large number of sheep farmers. In 1876 Henry Conway, a builder of Evershot, Dorset entered in his ledger:

3/- dozen hurdles. Sell for 7/-
1/- dozen slates[3]

The Davis family firm could deliver their hurdles for they purchased a lorry with solid tyres at an early date. In 1946 a two-ton Bedford lorry was purchased, which was usually driven by Montague, and in the spring of 1951 the family travelled to London and wove continuous fencing at the Festival of Britain.

As lambing time approached shepherds constructed lambing pens from hurdles. These were filled with hay and more hurdles were topped by a rough coat of thatch to form a roof. On exposed sites the sides of hurdles were also thatched to make an even warmer enclosure. Few sheep hurdles are used today.

Thatcher William Garrett of Trent recorded in his ledger for 20 March 1848:

Thatching of hurdles	1/-
Thatching 2 crebs [cribs]	1/6
2 cwt of spars	9d[4]

During March William Garrett also noted he made '35¼ Thousand of spars at 1/6 per thousand £2 – 12 – 10½'.[5] He usually charged farmers five shillings per thousand for long spars and four shillings per

thousand for short spars. Perhaps the 1/6 is the cost of cutting the gads for his use.

An alternative to sheep hurdles was sought as early as 1840 and in 1842 the Royal Agricultural Society of England awarded a sum of money to Messrs Wildey and Co. of Blackfriars, manufacturers of sheet netting, in the hope of producing a longer-lasting product. Other firms experimented with coconut fibre. The railway network did not reach the areas where most hurdles were made until 1857 to 1860 and before this time it was difficult to transport large hurdles easily. It had been hoped sheep netting would prove suitable in areas where there were few coppices. Twine netting was tried but it either shrank or went slack depending on the weather conditions. By 1850 iron hurdles were being made, with wheels fitted to help compensate for the extra weight. However, in areas where hurdlemakers worked steadily in productive coppices there seemed no need for change and many thousands of hurdles were made for sheep pens and temporary fencing to fold the sheep over root crops or pastures, which in turn manured the land. True sheep hurdles have a gap near the top which makes them more difficult to weave. A binder secures the lower weaving and after the gap a special weave called a twilley keeps the edge firm for further weaving. The sheep hurdles used to be supplied with a stick, called a shore, which was used to lift the hurdles through the gap and shift them to their new position. About four or five hurdles could be carried on a shore over the shoulder at any one time. Where hurdles were made thatching spars were made too. Barbed wire finally provided a cheap alternative for fencing rather than iron hurdles and netting.

Hazel has a wide variety of uses from gabions (containers filled with stones and used as fortifications) in war to fodder containers for cattle, as well as hurdles, baskets and spars. Gabions were made at the site of entrenchments in wartime. They would have proved light but bulky to transport empty and could quickly be made by many soldiers who had previously worked with hazel in their home villages. They must have served their purpose well.

Elaborate sheep cribs were often made by team effort and Sidney Davis made the hoops, with his sons constructing sides and rails. The ash from Oakers Wood was favoured for sheep cribs as it was an unusual ash with a white pimple in the bark and was exceptionally hard.

With today's revival of interest in thatch and thatched buildings there can be no doubt that the thatcher has a secure future, but the same cannot be said of the sparmaker and hurdlemaker. Fewer people today know what a spar is than 30 years ago although most thatched roofs contain several thousand of them. Hidden from sight their importance is not appreciated. Few people have seen the craftsmen at work and their numbers have declined steadily since the end of the First World War.

Some concern was expressed about the hazel underwood industry in 1950 and a detailed survey was carried out between 1952 and 1953. The results were published in a Forestry Commission Bulletin of 1956 and by that time numbers had dropped still further. 300 men were using only 12,200 of the 105,142 acres still available at that time. A few cut their crop on a six-year rotation but most preferred to wait nine to ten years.[6] After 1956 the worked area of hazel coppice shrank from 60,000 hectares to about 3,000. The Forestry Commission Census of Woodlands and Trees carried out between 1972 and 1982 showed the hectares of worked hazel coppice in England amounted to just 1,465 of hazel with standards and 1,573 hectares of pure hazel and 193 hectares of ash with standards and 1,184 of pure ash.[7]

Winter coppicing is far from a romantic occupation, for like that of the marsh reed harvester it starts after the first frost when the sap has retreated from the wood and the leaves have shrivelled. The woodsman works through the harshest of winter weather to provide the gads; they cannot be cut during the season of new growth. Hurdlemaker Sidney Donald Davis recalls that in frosty weather a split gad would be brittle, and shining with crystals. Efforts were sometimes made to thaw the gads by lighting fires in the coppices.

The time could soon arrive when there are not enough spars to satisfy demand. Even if all the neglected coppices were brought back into production, thick branches are impossible to split into slender spars by hand and no machine has been invented to do the job. The only modern change is that today's sparmaker will probably cut off his spar-gad lengths with an electric saw instead of a bow saw. As the demand for spars accelerates there is no way of speeding up the production process. At this stage it is uncertain whether young men will be tempted to take up the crafts of hurdlemaking and sparmaking and even if they do, it is not something they can learn overnight. The novice hurdlemaker and sparmaker is a cautious, slow worker unable to complete sufficient work to make a viable wage.

Just as the price of coppices has suffered from inflation so has the cost of spars. When Graeme Coombs started sparmaking in 1976 his first 5,000 spars realised £8 a thousand and he bought a new suit with his earnings! Today he estimates that he makes between 5,000 and 6,000 spars a week and in the 15 years it has been his full-time occupation he has only had one slack fortnight. The time taken to produce a bundle is often not known but an element of competition crept in a few years ago and a contest to produce a bundle of 250 spars from willow gads was easily won by Graeme Coombs in 40 minutes! The more usual rate would be in the region of 200 an hour. Today short spars

Reconstructed farmstead at the Weald and Downland Open Air Museum, Sussex.

The uses for hazel and willow have been numerous, from the simple fodder containers of peace to the gabions of war

can fetch £36 per thousand and longer spars £50 per thousand, with hazel liggers costing 14 to 15 pence each.

Spar length varies according to region and the roofing material being used. For centuries spars were either short, long or rick spars but today individual thatchers specify the exact length they prefer. The shortest produced by Graeme Coombs are only 20 in. (51 cm) long with an Oxford thatcher preferring 2 ft 2 in. (66 cm). Others ask for 2 ft 5 in. (69 cm) and some 2 ft 7 in.

(79 cm) with liggers up to 4 ft 6 in. (137 cm) long. Hurdlemakers and sparmakers still work in feet and inches.

Now that thatched roofs are once again in fashion, and executive thatched houses are being built, the new thatchers, without access to their own hazel coppices or the time to make their own spars while trying to carve out their thatching area in what has become a very competitive business, must soon look for an increase in the number of workers in the underwood.

4

House and home

From the time that the first threshing machine proved reasonably successful, in 1787, the craft of the thatcher was set to go into a gradual decline. His centuries of experimentation on roofs of all shapes and sizes had led to a large number of regional variations using many different thatching materials and all had proved successful if applied skilfully. However, there also still existed large numbers of hovels, housing two or three families, that many reformers considered unfit for habitation. Many others were damp and crumbling because their walls were not built on firm foundations and were soon to disappear or be demolished.

More substantial thatched houses, that had once been the home of prosperous yeoman farmers, had by this time been divided into labourers' cottages. Their former occupants were settling into square, purpose-built farmhouses, roofed in slates and tiles, situated in the centre of their freshly enclosed land. Improvements in communications, especially the spreading railway network, made it possible to bring Welsh slates to all areas at a competitive price. In 1873 52,000,000 slates were shipped from Porthmadog, the port that served the slate industry, and in 1882 the

Report of H.M. Inspector of Mines proudly declared 'after coal and iron, slate is the most valuable mineral raised in the U.K.'.

New thatched houses were not being built in any quantity but there were always some landowners who insisted on the vernacular style. Others left their individual mark on older thatched properties in an effort to turn a house into a home. Those who were not trying to survive on just a few shillings a week were seeking a picturesque effect and if unable to create a cottage orné, added a rustic porch and often a summerhouse in a corner of the garden.

The village priest had once lived in a thatched house next to his thatched church but from the beginning of the nineteenth century large brick and stone rectories began to appear, whose large roofs were unsuitable for thatching, which in any case would not have provided enough roof space for the large number of servants usually employed. However, the main reason for its decline in popularity was fashion.

Alteration was not always detrimental to the outward appearance. Glebe Cottage was an Elizabethan hall house built about 1560 with some cruck construction, and, surrounded by glebe land (i.e. land granted

Glebe Cottage, Thornford.

This cottage has seen change, especially during the nineteenth century, but its mixture of styles and materials only serves to enhance its charm

to the church), it seems likely that it was always designed to house the parish priest. It is a fine example of enlargement and improvement with an eye to the picturesque and this was achieved by using thatch. The cottage has two sets of roof timbers, making it unclear what the original roof covering was. Stone tiles have been dug up in the garden but as these were often laid at the eaves to shed water far away from the walls it cannot be assumed that stone tiles covered the whole roof; they were certainly not found in sufficient quantities. The back of the cottage is roofed in slates and the garage in tiles, which shows how both fashion and

availability influenced the owner's choice of materials but the mixture does not detract from the overall effect. The eye, however, is drawn to the thatched roof, which is in turn enhanced by the addition of a rustic wood and thatched porch. Even half-thatched roofs attract a premium and in 1989 the market price for this house was around £275,000.

Rectories were often built close to churchyard walls and so were the church ale houses. Many of these were thatched and thus provided periodic work for the thatchers who also worked on the ricks made from the tithe crops and crops from the glebe lands. After the Reformation the Puritans disapproved of the church ales that had helped boost the church income and although many ale houses were destroyed for this reason, a few survived to be converted into private houses, as at Manaton, Devon.

Other cottages were designed to house estate employees and serve as a feature near the entrance drives to large country houses. The Clifton Maybank restaurant attracts customers because of its small size, catslide roof and cottage atmosphere but few people realize the roof was not created with an eye to the picturesque. Originally built for the coachman/handyman at Clifton Maybank House it later became the chauffeur's house. A small extension resulted in a lower thatched roof that caught the full force of the rainwater shed by the main roof. A waterfall erodes the thatch after a few years, just as a natural waterfall would erode the stone beneath it, and to overcome the problem thatcher Archie Garrett built up the second roof until one continuous line of thatch ensured it all weathered at the same rate. Without its catslide the cottage would probably be passed without a second glance. It is a fine example of the practical becoming picturesque at a later date.

The restaurant, Clifton Maybank, Dorset.

The catslide roof was originally constructed for good thatching reasons and not for its picturesque effect

Ellwood's Stores, Thornford, Dorset.

A porch is more attractive when incorporated into the main thatched roof. The thatcher's individual interpretation enhances the character of this cottage

Porches were not original features on many cottages but added when materials became available or the tenant changed. Some porches were supported on rustic or brick framework while others were suspended as a canopy and did not always look attractive. The later thatched porch often deteriorated rapidly as few thatched roofs were fitted with gutters. It was the later skills of the thatcher that overcame problems like these. Just as the catslide roof makes a cottage appear more attractive today so can the skilful incorporation of the canopy of a porch into the main roof, with the added advantage that the thatch will

last longer. The thatcher, no doubt, enjoyed the opportunity to demonstrate his skills in this individual way. All of the adjacent thatched cottages at Thornford are built high above street level, necessitating steps up to the front door, and visitors think this was to escape flood water in the streets. From the rear it becomes apparent the gardens slope sharply down towards the houses. The raised height of the building overcame the problem of rainwater flooding the living accommodation but made it more difficult for the thatcher to reach the roof at the front. Sometimes a very long pole ladder was needed with over 40 rungs at ten inch

(25 centimetre) spacing. The thatcher's pole ladders were built with the sides reversed i.e. the curved edge of the split pole on the inside, which made them more comfortable to kneel on when working. Working from a ladder could lead to deformity in the feet in later years.

The coming of the railway to rural areas encouraged people to explore. For many it meant a first visit to the seaside, although the coast might be less than 20 miles (30 kilometres) away, and they were surprised to find different roofing styles. The railway created many problems for the thatcher: it gradually whittled away his work by introducing new materials and for others it provided alternative employment. Thatchers like Bill Guppy chose to give up their precarious existence in favour of regular and more comfortable work on the railway. Other thatchers, like Archie Garrett, took the opportunity of temporary employment on the railways in years when thatching materials were scarce. Cuttings were forged through the countryside, dividing farms and making access with a horse and cart difficult, especially when the barn storing the thatch was on one side of the line and the work on the other. Railway bridges were not low but when the longest pole ladder had to be carried it was essential to get the balance right and the horse had to be driven up the centre of the road to enable the ladder to clear the underside of the bridge. Only the thatcher's cart was designed to take such a long ladder and the last cart made for one family cost less than £12 in 1912.

A high sprung cart was essential for the thatcher, for although he rarely had large quantities of reed to carry he did supply his own tools, spars and ladders. The height was calculated so that a long pole ladder would clear the ground at the back and rest sufficiently far above the horse's head at the front not to prove a distraction. There was an art to raising such a long ladder and it

was a two-man operation. The first thatcher put up a shorter pole ladder to eaves level and climbed up balancing the end of the long ladder on his shoulder. When in position both thatchers pushed from ground level and the ladder could be rolled over to reach another course on the roof without the full weight having to be lifted again, and then could safely be left in position at night. Other thatchers balanced shorter pole ladders in the bed of the wagon that had brought their long-straw thatch when extra height was needed.

The railway also brought supplies of corrugated iron sheets and many farmers

Once a separate cottage, now part of the Manor House, Yetminster, Dorset.

Galvanized iron sheets provided a cheap replacement roof covering at a time when cost mattered more than appearance

used them as a cheap form of roofing material. Many cottages lost their character although the sheets might well be sculpted to follow the original roof line. Often, a cement fillet on the chimney stack, high above the new roof level, gives a clue to a cottage that once had a thatched roof. As agricultural profits fell and farmers faced a time of insecurity it is hardly surprising that they opted for a roof covering for cottages and barns that worked out at half the price of thatch. In some areas where thatchers were hard to find it was the only alternative. Only now are these roofs having their thatch restored. Thatch has better insulating properties and is far quieter to live underneath than corrugated iron. In some cases the corrugated sheets were fixed over the remaining thin layer of thatch, but in cases of fire it hindered the firemen. They found that their poles, that could quickly pull off the burning thatch, were useless and when the new roof became red hot there was little they could do to save the cottage. In 1989 over half of the thatched work undertaken in Britain was on new roofs, extensions and the replacement of thatch on roofs such as these.

In Wales few new thatched properties have appeared yet, but the signs are encouraging, and in 1989 Peter Brugge thatched a rebuilt and much enlarged house at Llangollen for the first time. In 1949 there were still some thatched roofs in Prestatyn High Street, but in Rhuddlan most of the thatch had disappeared under galvanized corrugated iron sheets by this date; the few survivors are now features of the landscape. One thatched house stands at the top of Ffardd Isa in Prestatyn and the thatched-house café on the St Asaph to Denbigh road is picturesque, attracting trade because it has retained its thatch. Today in Wales, as in other areas, there is a mixture of styles, with some houses thatched in Norfolk reed and others in imported reed. Long-straw thatch had been common in the more fertile areas of Wales such as the Vale of Glamorgan and parts of Clwyd. In West Wales a technique known as thrust thatching was the local style, where bundles of straw were 'thrust' into an underthatch rather than being laid on the roof in courses. Today, examples of thrust thatch can be seen at the Welsh Folk Museum at St Fagans. Slate had also replaced thatch on roofs in North Wales but at least one cottage has now had its thatched roof reinstated and no doubt more will follow.

It was estimated that thatched hovels were only replaced by more substantial dwellings in a ratio of one to three. In some areas, where much of the rural population had drifted to the towns, this was sufficient, but in others it led to serious overcrowding. Sometimes the thatchers moved into the towns too. William Garrett was born into a thatching family but left Dorset to become a blacksmith in the London area before taking his family to Australia. William Bear confirmed the housing shortage in 1893: 'The chief cause of the shortness of supply is the demolition of old and bad cottages without a corresponding erection of new ones'; and also stated that 'the great majority are of brick and tile'. The Duke of Bedford, he found, had replaced many old cottages with larger properties but only in the above ratio.

Turnpike cottages often provided accommodation for homeless families, and removed them from parish relief by providing them with useful employment as gatekeepers. This was not always the case, but these purpose-built cottages were far superior to the many hovels that still existed at this time. The Snowdon Turnpike cottage lies at the fork of the steep Snowdon Hill and the road to Wambrook in Somerset, and was last lived in eight years ago. Built in 1839 by the Chard Turnpike Trust when a loop road was opened to avoid the steep Snowdon Hill, it was called 'The Round House' but was in fact polygonal. The

The Snowdon Turnpike cottage, Chard, Somerset.
This cottage displays a variety of architectural styles. Its Gothic arches and studded door contrast with the rustic verandah

single-storey flint walling is topped by a combed wheat-reed roof and despite its pointed, arched windows with Gothic glazing bars and studded door it is unlikely to have been expensive to build. The projecting eaves, supported by round wooden poles, form a verandah. Nestling into the hillside the thatch has resisted the weather well. Toll-gates were not popular, and avoided if possible, but this one was a well-used route carrying overseas mail to

Devon and Cornwall to avoid the longer sea route up the English Channel. The last tenant, Mrs Jewell, was the daughter of the Price family who had lived at the turnpike cottage for many years.

In 1985 Chard celebrated 750 years of borough life based on the 1851 Census Return by acting out episodes of bygone days. One scene featured the courting of 14-year-old Lois Mitchem, the daughter of Widow Mitchem, the Snowdon toll-gate keeper and was researched by Mr Len Hoskins. He was sad to find she did not marry her suitor but died at the age of 22 and was the first person to be buried in the new cemetery.

Not every widow was as fortunate as Mrs Mitchem for many ended their days in the poor-house. The Sputel poor-houses were thatched hovels and no one was sorry when they were demolished before the First World War and carts of stone from them were seen being carried through local villages. Another thatched poor-house was built at Holbrook, Dorset and seems to have kept the local thatcher busy, for the policy to repair and not re-thatch completely saved parish funds

from any single enormous bill (although the number of small bills made this practice a false economy).

In 1772 Thomas Brake was paid £3 13s 6d for thatching the Poor House at Holbrook and a further £2 17s 9d later that year for repair work. Reed sheaves had cost four pence each and 50 were required.

At Batcombe four small houses were provided for the poor and more poor occupied Row Cottage. Thatching and repairs cost the parish £6 12s 4d between 1830 and 1846.[1]

In the 1890s photographer Francis Frith and his trained assistants visited many towns and villages throughout the country

Thatchways, Iwerne Minster, Dorset, 1912.

Thatchways, photographed soon after the *Titanic* sank, was designed by a man with an eye to the future

to make picture postcards at a time when the picture postcard could be sent at half the letter rate of a penny. At Ringwood in Hampshire, Frith recorded the long-straw thatcher at work on his pole ladder of over 40 rungs, setting an idyllic scene with a river frontage. However the thatcher is already struggling to work around a galvanized sheeted extension. Another Frith postcard taken at Dorchester, Dorset shows the more usual thatch of the day with freshly applied patches, and a new ridge with the remaining coat decaying under a coat of moss.

The *Western Gazette* reported on 25 October 1889 that 'Very heavy weather was experienced on this part of the coast on Friday night and early Saturday Morning. In several instances chimney tops have been blown down and a great many slates and tiles displaced'. A long section of recently constructed wall was also blown down but there is no mention of damage to thatch or ricks as would have dominated such news 50 years before.

'Much has happened in the world of housing since 1913,' Lawrence Weaver stated when he prepared his second edition of the *Country Life Book of Cottages* in 1919. After the First World War, high costs and shortages of materials revived the quest for the cheap but well-constructed houses that had started at the turn of the century. It was agreed there was 'the need to provide cottages of a sort that shall not disfigure the countryside'[2] and attempts were made to build a cottage for £150 exclusive of site.

The competition for designs for Letchworth Garden City had been well supported but resulted in a large number 'of cottages which were freakish or unsatisfactory in design or material'. The first prize was awarded to Mr Percy Hougton for a cottage that appeared to meet the requirements but it was not thatched. A challenge was issued to architects to better the design of Mr St Loe Strachey's (a contemporary campaigner for housing

reform) and this was taken up by Arnold Mitchell who, in October 1913, published particulars of a pair of cottages at Merrow that had cost £220. The *Country Life* National Competition followed in 1914, after a great deal of public indignation in 1913 about the destruction of a cottage by 'a well-known college' which was replaced with 'a building of unusual ugliness'. Thus roused, a number of well-known people got together and 18 landowners throughout the country agreed to build at least a pair of cottages from a selection of the first prize winners in each category. Efforts were made to reach a high standard with regard to regional house styles.

The President of the Board of Agriculture, the Rt Hon. Walter Runciman, opened the public exhibition by paying tribute to the services of *Country Life* in promoting the competition, referring to them as 'the keeper of architectural conscience of the U.K.'. Already it was realized that the labourer was seeking a parlour and separate kitchen and the designs had been submitted bearing this in mind, with a cost limit set at £250 per pair for the smallest. One of the competitors, Mr Christopher Turnor, admitted he did not expect anyone to be able to build to his design for less than £295 the pair. Mr Courtney Crickmer's design for the cheapest type of cottages gained a second place to Mr Harvey's and it was noted Mr Harvey's design provided 725 superficial feet (i.e. surface area) of floor space for £150 compared to Joseph Gandy's 470 feet for a design in 1805 costing the same price. More pleasing designs were submitted and Mr Raymond Unwin's 'very interesting thatched bungalow of charming appearance' at Hollesley Bay drew praise but was built at the low pre-war cost of £220.

An attractive group of four thatched cottages was built to C.R. Ashbee's designs at Catbrook, Gloucester and another group of thatched cottages was built at Ashby St Ledgers, Northamptonshire, designed by Sir

Edwin Lutyens for Lord Wimborne. They were described as having thick thatched roofs 'with admirable dormers and ridge, the unbroken roof-line and the stout brick chimneys produce an effect altogether picturesque and satisfactory'.[3]

'Thatchways' (p. 82) at Iwerne Minster met nothing but praise from *Country Life*: 'delightful examples. Mr James H. Ismay has done much towards preserving the ancient character of the village'. The cottages were described as being 'markedly superior to what can be expected from landowners in the ordinary way'.[4]

However James Hainsworth Ismay, who retired from Ismay, Imrie & Co. (the ship owning company best known for its White Star Line) in 1902 at the early age of 32, due to ill-health, was seeking something special. His agent, Rawlence, finally found a thatching family who were expert combed wheat-reed thatchers as he did not want the local long-straw style, but they lived at the other end of the county. In the days of the horse and cart it was the railway that enabled them to accept the offer of work which was very welcome in a year of shortages of materials after the disastrous long dry summer of 1911. The thatchers knew it would be wise to accept if they could overcome the problems of materials and transport. Crop failure had not been as widespread in Devon and the enterprising thatchers managed to get supplies delivered to the site. All that remained was to obtain accommodation near the new houses and arrange their own transport. The horse was harnessed to the shafts and the cart was loaded with spars, ladders and tools and the thatchers were driven to the station by a nephew. The porter joked as he loaded everything into a goods wagon, for it was the first time he had seen thatchers going to work by train.

Thatchways was originally built as two cottages with another matching pair in the village, and they provided roomy accommodation. Ismay's aim had been not only to improve his estate, but also to provide extra accommodation for workers at his new bacon factory, where his manufacture was aimed at large liners such as the *Titanic* and *Olympic*. Returning home at the end of each week the thatchers were met with the horse and cart stabled at a safe distance (the arrival of the steam train frightened many horses). When the thatchers returned to work on Monday 15 April 1912 they were unaware that the *Titanic* had sunk that morning. When news filtered through that Joseph Bruce Ismay, James Ismay's elder brother and manager of the White Star Line, had survived, both the estate workers and the thatchers were surprised that it was a thanksgiving service at the local church they were expected to attend and not a memorial service for all the lives that had been lost.

James Hainsworth Ismay died in 1930 and his obituary praised his contributions to agriculture and the improvement of the countryside. It was realized, however, that he had had the income to interpret his vision without thinking of the return.

Mr Ismay was not thinking of an economic rent, but of the amenities of the village. It may be hoped that there will still be landowners who can afford to wink at a low return on capital expenditure and follow such a good example.

He devoted himself with open-handed generosity to the welfare of his tenants, and the cottagers on his estate will long lament the passing of so benevolent an owner.[5]

Today, Thatchways is one large house that boasts four reception rooms, six bedrooms and two bathrooms, in landscaped gardens of just under an acre. It was sold *c.* 1985 for £140,000. In 1990 the price was £310,000.

Bladen Valley saw a lifetime's association between Sir Ernest Debenham and the Fooks family of thatchers. Sir Ernest's love of thatch was evident throughout the whole

Bladen Valley, Briantspuddle, Dorset.

Bladen Valley taxed the thatchers' creativity with a wide variety of roof styles. The walls were constructed of large concrete cavity blocks cast on the site using an experimental Swedish machine

of his estate, and a great deal of his wealth was invested in preserving and improving the village of Briantspuddle; he even insisted the village hall was thatched. He then turned his attention to the Bladen Valley, half a mile away, where he spent a number of years overseeing the building of his new hamlet, working with Halsey Ricardo of the building contractors Ricardo Ltd and the architect MacDonald Gill. Both Ricardo and MacDonald Gill worked hard with the thatchers to interpret varied designs for cottages at a reasonable cost while providing generous living accommodation. Work began soon after war broke out and was not completed until 1920 when a war memorial,

a major work by sculptor Eric Gill in white Portland stone-said to be the most beautiful war memorial in Great Britain – was added at the entrance to the hamlet. Sir Ernest Debenham's model village also drew praise from *Country Life*, who kept the location of Bladen Valley a secret.

Close inspection of the cottages reveals conventional materials were not used for the walls. The cottage appearance, with every conceivable style of thatched roof and a pleasing colour to the walls, fools many into thinking stone was used. Halsey Ricardo, in fact, experimented with an imported Swedish machine that cast very large, hollow concrete blocks on site, using local gravel in the mixture to give it a golden shade. However, it was found that despite the large cavity, the walls still proved porous and had to be coated with a layer of cement plaster to damp-proof them. One eight-roomed cottage providing office accommodation for an estate worker at the entrance to the Bladen Valley was praised for its low construction cost of only £147.

Thatchers John and Alan Fooks, from a family with a thatching history dating back at least 300 years, believed the hamlet was based on Milton Abbas, but a more imaginative design, with trees planted between the varied cottage styles. Others claim similarities with John Nash's Blaise Hamlet.

Alan Fooks continued to thatch at Bladen Valley until his retirement, using a Landrover and trailer in later years. (His father and grandfather had used a pony and trap.) He began his thatching career at the age of nine, when his first job was to put the points on the spars which were split by his father. He also recalls how on Saturday mornings he had to draw bundles of thatch from a straw rick ready for long-straw thatching the following week. They used tar twine to secure the bundles to the new roofs and cut their own spar gads from hazel and willow. He added, 'Today it's all felt and barge crooks'!

Sir Ernest Debenham realised the problems in finding a supply of thatching materials and both he and another local farmer used to grow wheat reed for the thatchers, that was then stored in a thatched rick. Sometimes Alan Fooks and his father undertook other thatching work in south Dorset using Abbotsbury 'spear' or marsh reed.

Mr Anthony Pearman wrote of rural industries soon after the Second World War. Of thatching he felt,

there is more in it than meets the eye; the shaping of gable ends, delicately clothing out-peeping dormer windows, and carefully following the lines of

swelling and receding curves, all require the artist's understanding, and the craftsman's skill.[6]

He could not have chosen truer words.

Jerrards North and South were designed at a time when few were thinking of building new thatched cottages, yet in rural areas thatch was the sensible choice of roof covering and still readily available in 1930. The village thatcher was not invited to undertake the work but instead it went to a thatching family living five miles (eight kilometres) away who had just purchased a new Morris Tourer. Perhaps Tom Martin's liking for drink had precluded him from being offered the work, but although he often arrived late in the morning he would then work steadily and well. The thatchers invited him to help thatch the cottages but he was paid his earnings in two parts: a weekly wage, and the balance when the work was completed, for fear he would disappear before the work was finished. Everyone seemed happy with the arrangement. The cottages were situated not far from the long drive to Jerrards, a house that boasted a thatched Elizabethan barn and a thatched stable block in the style of William and Mary. All were kept in good order until recent years but today the roof of the stable block has collapsed.

Even recently substantial thatched cottages have continued to be demolished. In the mid-nineteenth century, when the young Banger family moved to 'Latts Sulls', a limestone cottage with a thatched roof of long straw, it was considered a substantial cottage of its day. It was not large, but several generations of Bangers were raised there and it was far from Richard Heath's descriptions of country homes of agricultural labourers that he wrote in 1870:

the majority of cottages that exist in rural parishes are deficient in almost every requisite that should constitute a home. [The commissioners of 1867 found] *tumbledown and ruinous, not water-tight* [cottages everywhere. In Norfolk the

Jerrards Cottages, Sandford Orcas, Dorset.

Jerrards North and South were not constructed until 1930, by which time few estates were insisting new cottages should be thatched

cottages were] *both shocking and scandalous* [and in Buckinghamshire were] *wretched hovels.*

However, despite being built of stone from the local quarry without porous walls, and having the later additions of a brick chimney stack and porch, Latts Sulls was demolished after the Second World War to make way for an estate of council houses. Many cottages of character that would be lovingly restored today were lost between 1930 and 1960.

At the time the Banger family moved to Latts Sulls one literate thatcher, William Garrett, kept a detailed ledger that has survived. Although much of his work centred around the village farms at Trent, Dorset he sometimes undertook general thatching. In 1851 he billed the Rev. W.H. Turner of Trent for thatching his stable:

£1	5s	6d	
	16s	0d	*for 4,000 spars at 4/- per*
£2	1s	6d	*thousand*

Home-grown materials were supplied by the owner of the property with the thatcher providing just labour and spars. Shortly afterwards William billed Mrs Custard '£1 13s 3d for work done' to her cottage. Sometimes he provided the materials for he billed the Trustees of Trent School for minor repairs:

1 sq. 0 feet of thatching at 3/-	3s	0d
2 reed sheaves at 7d per sheaf	1s	2d
1 quarton of spars	1s	0d
	5s	2d[7]

Spars were usually bundled into 250s at this date, so since he charged the Rev. Turner four shillings per thousand spars, it would seem that only one bundle was needed, which would have taken him less than two hours to make. Although the amounts seem small William was his own master and his cash receipts would have far exceeded the few shillings a week that agricultural labourers were paid at this time. For example, when James Phippen, an agricultural labourer in the neighbouring parish of Hendford, married Lucy Singleton in 1885 they had to survive on eight shillings a week and when woodsman George Gray married their daughter, Elizabeth Phippen, in 1908 his weekly wage was 15 shillings. Unlike thatcher William Garrett their hours were fixed, as were their wages, with no occasional cash influxes that might have allowed them to take advantage of any bargains to improve their lot.

A far less substantial cottage than Latts Sulls occupied a small piece of ground on the edge of a village allotment field and was once occupied by 'Aunt Polly' Hatcher, the widow of an infamous poacher who was reputed 'to run like the wind and jump like a deer'. Despite his many escapades he was never caught. In her younger days Aunt Polly used to walk five miles (eight kilometres) each way to the nearest coaching inn, The Quicksilver Mail, with pheasants tied around her waist beneath her full skirts. In later years she lived with her cat in the one-roomed thatched hovel where her great niece used to sit on a stool counting the spiders that crept amongst the thatch and rafters (the cottage had no ceiling). A few years later a rumble was heard by the village thatcher as he worked on his allotment and the roof of Aunt Polly's cottage fell in; the thin layer of thatch had not been able to hold the rotting hedge-pole roof up any longer. Luckily, a short time before the old lady had moved to another thatched cottage that has since been demolished.

The Society for the Protection of Ancient Buildings was formed in 1876 thanks to the foresight of men such as John Ruskin, Thomas Carlyle and William Morris, but it gave no protection at that time to cottages

Latts Sulls, Oborne, Dorset, *c.* 1900.

The later additions of a brick chimney stack and porch did not prevent Latts Sulls being demolished in the 1940s

such as these. The first State step, The Ancient Monuments Act of 1882, gave protection to a few monuments but not to churches or houses. The majority of historic buildings, whether occupied or empty, received no protection until the Town and Country Planning Act of 1947, which was too late for many buildings. Even after this date some were lost because their isolated positions were unrecorded and they had never received the protection of a listed building.

Whitewashed cob walls covered by rolling coats of combed wheat reed is the vernacular of Devon, where it was usual to leave the roofs unwired against bird damage. Broadhembury is one of Devon's most picturesque villages and owes its preservation to the Drewe family, who purchased a large proportion of the parish in the 1950s and some before that date, and would not allow it to be altered. Philip Tilden thatched the cottages for Sir Cedric Drewe who had them restored when he bought them. Recently however, just outside the centre of the village some new houses

Broadhembury, Devon.

Broadhembury owes its preservation to one family who would not allow change in the 1950s. On the village outskirts a mixture of thatching materials can be seen

Leap Cottage, Trent, Dorset.

Leap Cottage is not a particularly imaginative design but was constructed in the 1960s when few people regarded thatch as a modern roofing material

Abbotsbury, Dorset.

This imposing new house was built of local materials. Local marsh reed over stone walls help blend it into its surroundings. It was built *c.* 1985

have been built, and although they do have thatched roofs they are not of combed wheat reed but imported marsh reed which does not harmonize with the rest of the village.

Leap Cottage, Trent caused much excitement when it was built 25 years ago for it was to have a thatched roof. Although it is not the most picturesque design for a

house a great deal of thought went into its construction. Just as James Hainsworth Ismay, Sir Ernest Debenham and the Jerrards Estate had specified their new houses should have thatched roofs over 35 years before, so in each decade there seems to have been someone who has let their feelings dictate against the current trend.

Opposite Leap Cottage is a small, tastefully converted cider barn that has retained its thatched roof. Earlier this century the Trent thatcher, Alban Gillard, would probably have worked on this roof. He was one of the few left-handed thatchers and when working with a right-handed thatching family he had to work on the opposite side of the roof to them. Two right-handed thatchers can each thatch a course on the same side of the roof. Alban worked well but had to have left-handed shearing hooks made for him by the blacksmith.

In 1985 it was decided to build a new house at Abbotsbury, a village where thatch predominates and local marsh reed is grown. Careful planning and a thatched roof of local 'spear' reed was the correct choice. If villages have to expand, a great deal of thought should be given not only to the individual design but to the overall effect on the appearance of the village.

Redundant barns are not the only buildings that are considered desirable for conversion. All over the country there are redundant buildings that once played an important role in a self-sufficient village. However, few craftsmen work in villages today. Church Cottage at Mudford in Somerset was converted in the early 1980s and is a cottage with an interesting history. It once formed part of a blacksmith's and wheelwright's complex and is situated close to the ford where they had a convenient

Church Cottage, Mudford, Somerset.

Described by the owners as looking 'like a sugar loaf' this cottage has an interesting history and once formed part of a blacksmith's complex. Thatch covered by pantiles has now been restored but using imported Austrian marsh reed

Abbots Mede, Formby, near Liverpool.

Fairclough Homes found their decision to offer a selection of executive homes with thatched roofs popular in 1989. More thatched properties will be included in future developments

source of water. It has been described by the present owners as looking 'like a sugar loaf' and they found it difficult to decide what its original use had been, although they believe it may have been the blacksmith's store. There was an external staircase and a fireplace that seemed far too large for a cottage of this size. A photograph taken in 1891 showed a thatched roof and a family standing outside. However, at some date pantiles (overlapping roof tiles) were fastened directly to the remaining thin thatched coat and these remained in place until the cottage was restored. Originally it would have been an easy cottage to thatch, with no height problem for the thatcher to

overcome. The choice would have been long straw and perhaps at a later date combed wheat reed. Today it is thatched in imported Austrian reed and has had windows and a door inserted in the wall facing the road.

When thatch was considered the poor man's roofing material no-one would have thought of building executive houses with thatched roofs. However, once a thatched house appeared at the Ideal Homes Exhibition for the first time it was possible to contemplate building thatched properties simply because they were different and desirable in their own right. Abbots Mede, an estate of 11 houses at Formby near

Liverpool, was described as 'Homes in Harmony with Nature', each built to a 'time-honoured maturity of style, interpreted through modern materials and technology'. It was possible to vary the roof designs and include intricate patterns in the thatching. In 1989 Fairclough Homes could have sold treble the number of thatched houses they had built and immediately decided to incorporate thatched houses on other estates. No doubt Fairclough Homes's decision will persuade other developers to follow suit. The overall effect was completed by the addition of a village green and pond, landscaped with ornamental trees and shrubs. A modern interpretation of John Nash's Blaise Hamlet perhaps!

Ornamental shapes cut into the outer layers of the reed at different stages can be seen today in many areas where marsh reed has been used, especially on new houses where the picturesque is especially

This new house at Fontmell Magna was completed in 1989.

Thatched houses are moving away from traditional designs

New thatched cottages at Abbotsbury, Dorset.

Although marsh reed is grown in the village of Abbotsbury, imported reed was used on these cottages, completed in 1990

desirable. These sorts of shapes were first introduced in the last decades of the nineteenth century by the Farman family of Norfolk, who boast a thatching history in excess of 300 years. Based near Salhouse, Norfolk they also introduced the fashion of 'herring-boning' in place of 'diamonding', using split hazel lengths. Today, as in so many of the established thatching families, there are no young direct heirs to carry on the family tradition.

The modern thatched house does not have to be a period piece. It can still look attractive if built of brick with modern windows and with no prctcncc of bclonging

to a past age. A detached house at Fontmell Magna, Dorset is but one of many such houses appearing all over the country. This house stands a short distance from a low, sixteenth-century thatched cottage, and although the two are in complete contrast to each other the new thatched house seems somehow to complement the older property. It will become a desirable family home.

Bricks can be chosen today without the restrictions of the brick tax introduced in 1784. To help get round the problem of a tax that was calculated on the number of bricks used and not the volume of the brickwork, large bricks were produced measuring up to 10 × 5 × 3 in. (25.4 × 12.7 × 7.6 cm). In 1803, a further tax was levied on these large bricks but could be circumvented by reducing the size slightly. The brick tax was finally removed in 1850, but by that time ready supplies of slates and tiles were at hand and were the more usual choice to cover the new brick walls.

Not all new thatched cottages are designed to be executive period homes or are obviously built to a modern design. A terrace of houses completed in 1990 appeared at first glance to be a barn conversion but a conversation with the builders revealed that the barn that had originally stood on the site had been carefully demolished and the stone used to build a large thatched house. The terrace of cottages built of new stone will be indistinguishable from the surrounding period cottages in a few years time. However, although marsh reed is grown locally and was used on the surrounding properties that sport combed wheat-reed ridges, imported reed from Holland was used here. Just as thatchers in Norfolk protested when it was proposed a church should be re-thatched in imported reed so perhaps the time has come when villages should insist local materials are used when they are available. However, if they are in short supply, any thatching material must be preferable to the adoption of designs quite alien to their surroundings.

5

The farm

Most farmers today have little use for the thatcher's craft. Villages that earlier this century contained as many as 15 farms may now have two at the most and sometimes none at all. New agricultural machinery, changes of use and farming methods have all taken their toll of traditional farm buildings, many of which were not protected in any way. The farmyard that contained the granary, threshing barn, stables, dairy, cheese room, wagon and cow sheds, and rick barton has no place in modern agriculture. Where farms have survived their structure has changed and two men work on the acreage that once employed 18 labourers. Access has had to be made for combine harvesters, milk tankers, cattle lorries and large tractors pulling implements of unprecedented size.

Thatch somewhere on the farm was once almost inevitable, for even if the farmhouse was not thatched most other shelters were. The thatcher was as important to the farmer for providing the protection required for animals, machinery, food crops and man as the farmer was to the thatcher, supplying him with over 80 per cent of his annual work and his thatching materials.

Today the thatcher is the man that creates the picturesque from the dilapidated and the ugly. As little as 50 years ago he was the man who executed the essential repairs and 100 years ago the thatcher's complete round would often be between the farms of his home village. The practical uses of thatch were numerous, although many roof coverings were only required for a short period of time. The farming year occupied the thatcher's thoughts and there was little opportunity for him to experiment with the ornamental. A complete new coat of thatch was rare and only carried out when there was no other way of completing a weatherproof covering. Economics always won over the picturesque.

Conversion has turned the most ruinous shells of former working barns into desirable residences, and in some areas no farm barns of any age are left unaltered. However, there will always be a few who take pride in the appearance of their farmyards and preserve the outer façade wherever possible while others turn a blind eye and let vernacular buildings decay.

Manor farms were often the largest in a village and once the hub of village life. The Manor Farm at Melbury Osmond has fallen into decay in recent years and the thatch on the large farmhouse roof is in a far more

Manor farmhouse and cottage, Melbury Osmond, Dorset.

Decaying farmyards are a sad sight. The half-hipped small building is in a better state of preservation than the manor farmhouse roof but the whole is strangely silent and empty

advanced stage of decay than that of a half-hipped thatched building nearby that once provided living accommodation for a labourer and his family. The farmyard is equally decayed and the shell of a burnt-out thatched barn marks the end of an era. This farm alone would have created enough work for a thatcher and the small village provided full-time employment for three in 1851. By 1954, E.J. Stowe noted: 'Few, if any, farmers construct roofs of thatch nowadays'.[1]

Thatch began disappearing from farm buildings at a much earlier date in the north and farmhouses in Aberdeen were beginning to sport slated roofs from 1740. However, traditional Scottish long houses retained their thatch of heather for many more years. Further south smaller farms kept their thatch for economic reasons as they produced their own thatching materials.

Farmer Stacey of Trent turned his attention to the state of his farmhouse roof in May 1853. Thatcher William Garrett had to cut the gads, make the spars and thatch the farmhouse but his materials were supplied for him. The 'sqr' was a roof area of 10 × 10 feet (3 × 3 metres).

5 sq 72 feet thatching Mr Stacey's at	
3/- per sqr	16/6
Cutting out of Spar Gads	3/0

[Mr Stacey was also billed for]

2 Swedy graves	2/6
3 Mangel graves	2/6
1 stub mow [stubble]	1/-
1 load of peas	1/-
thatching hurdles and	
1 lb. of twine	1/-
1 Pursnip Cave	2/6
1 Mangel Cave	1/6

as well as for thatching 48 ricks, '1 potato cave, 1 Sweed Cave, thatch to hurdles and thatch to 1 Sacket Mow'.

William Garrett's ledger provides a great deal of information about a typical village thatcher's life from the middle of the nineteenth century. He was literate, methodical and, in flowing handwriting, recorded his work in minute detail. His ledger is rare because few others have survived. William's spelling errors are consistent so there was a distinct difference between a grave, cave and barrow.

Lower Farm, Yetminster, Dorset.

Lower Farm is being sympathetically restored and will remain part of an active village farm. Thatched dormers and attractive eyebrow windows to the rear produce changing angles that test the skill of Rural Development Commission apprentice thatcher Dan Munro

Bradford Abbas, Dorset.

The life of the thatched roof of this disused cow byre has been extended by sparring on a thin layer of new thatch, once common practice on all roofs

thatching 2 sweed grave in barrows 2/-[2]

In contrast to Manor Farm, Lower Farm, in a neighbouring village, was given a new lease of life by a farming family in 1988. Home grown Aquila combed-wheat thatching reed was harvested by an Albion binder pulled by a tractor of a similar age. The combination worked well on the organic field. Mobile threshing tackle fitted with a reed comber produced the thatcher's reed which was then stored in a rick. New roof timbers were required, to replace the originals that dated from 1707, and were covered with impervious felt. The thatch was fixed into place with steel rods and crooks instead of spars, which were only used on the ridge. Today, thatchers are often required to work from scaffolding for insurance purposes.

Not all farm buildings were located next to the farmhouse or barton. Cow byres were often built in small pasture fields, but as dairy herds increased in number and milking methods changed many became redundant and have already been

Manor Farm Barn, Thornford, Dorset.

Manor Farm Barn still plays an important role in the working life of this farm at Thornford. Its new coat of combed wheat reed will protect it for another 30 years

demolished. Too small for implement sheds and often surrounded today by a ploughed field more of these attractive buildings will no doubt be lost.

Gale damage often produced a spate of work for the thatcher and the spring of 1870 was no exception. Farmer Stacey was billed for:

Repering laming house	5/-
Righting Dog House	1/-
Thatching Dogs House	2/6[3]

The farm dog was a working dog and always housed outside. The cost for thatching his shelter was equivalent to that of thatching a small rick so his house must have been substantial. Dog House Farm at Sherborne, Dorset, took its name from a similar substantial shelter at its entrance.

Some barns are not neglected and will always be an important feature of the farmyard. Manor Farm Barn at Thornford still serves a useful purpose today. It once had a central arch through which access was gained to the farmyard beyond. One year the barn was so full of grain that the

101

pressure caused a wall to collapse and with it part of the thatched roof. The thatcher had to remove loose thatch and wire netting without disturbing the firm sections of the roof and the wall was rebuilt, but without the attractive archway. In the summer of 1988 5.8 tonnes of Aquila combed-wheat reed were stored in the barn and removed as the thatcher needed it and the roof contains over 10,000 hazel spars. The adjoining granary has a slate roof and here farmer Caleb Ryall hosted the First World War peace celebrations in 1919.

1958			
Coating back of barn. 11½ sq. at 50/- per sq.	£28	15.	0.
Tying in undercoat, tarred twine and labour	£5	0.	0.
4,500 spars at 50/- per 1,000	£11	5.	0.
1960			
Coating front and part of back of barn 21½ sq. at 55/-	£59	2.	6.
8,000 spars at £3. 5. 0. per 1,000	£26	0.	0.
	£130	2.	6.[4]

Today the combed wheat reed cost £450 per tonne plus VAT and the total cost exceeded £5,000.

Some granaries were thatched but many are redundant today. The Weald and Downland Open Air Museum rebuilt an unusually large example that measures 20 feet (6 metres) square. In 1731 the roof covering would have been long-straw thatch but today it has a roof of combed wheat reed that was virtually unknown to Sussex until recently and it is estimated to be its twelfth coat of thatch. Reed thatch from the estuaries would have vied with long straw in this area as the most popular thatching material. When it was usual to add new thatch on top of a firm old coat the thickness could be considerable; a workshop roof was removed at Abbotsbury recently and the local marsh reed underneath was found to be six feet (1.8 metres) thick. The building was dated according to the local tradition that a new coat of one foot (30 cm) depth was required every 60 years!

After the enclosure acts removed land from those who could not prove their entitlement to it, small cottages sprang up on wide verges, unenclosed heaths, commons and crossroads and became a national problem. Large farmers often profited from the enclosures but few small self-sufficient farmers had documentary proof of ownership. At Lake, in Dorset, Honeycomb Cottage is one of the finest surviving examples of this type of dwelling that originally consisted of two small rooms. Once, 17 cottages of the cultivated strips survived within this parish where little effort

The Littlehampton Granary, Weald and Downland Open Air Museum, Sussex.

Thatched granaries are becoming rare as changing agricultural methods make them obsolete on the modern farm. This granary was easily accessible from all sides and posed little problem for the thatcher to complete

Thatcher Simon Garrett working at Honeycombe Cottage, Lake, Dorset.

The thatcher tackles the small roof of Honeycombe Cottage, built on a wide verge, by using two short roofing ladders fixed into the thatch by long spikes. His reed holder is home-made and effective. The small-gauge wire that hangs in rolls at the eaves will be replaced to prevent birds nesting in the new combed wheat-reed thatch

was made, perhaps for compassionate reasons, to have them demolished. With the front elevation facing west the end hipped walls almost fit the verge exactly, leaving long tapering garden strips to the front and rear. Cottages sprang up overnight in the firm belief that if a chimney stack was built between dawn and dusk and a fire lit in the hearth by nightfall, ownership was confirmed. Although it was not a legal practice many such cottages do survive. Today the roof is of combed wheat reed fastened with hazel spars and is protected by a coat of small gauge wire mesh.

Although the farmers of the strips brought little work for the thatcher other farms created a vast assortment of tasks. It was common practice not to submit a bill until the end of each season so the thatcher had to have sufficient funds to survive until then, but once the bill was paid he had surplus cash to invest in a cow, calves, sheep or pigs.

Larger landowners often paid quarterly or six-monthly. William Garrett billed the farmers of Trent each spring. Thatchers were not uneducated, illiterate or simple, as portrayed by the lampooners. William Garrett, a working man in 1847, had obviously received some formal education long before many villages had a national school and was as knowledgeable of the field names as the farmer himself.

In February 1847 he submitted a bill to Mr G. Genge.

	£	s	d
Thatching 6 mow stadles in Barton		6	
Making 15 thousands of spars at 1/6	1	2	6
Thatching 2 hay ricks in Barton		7	
Thatching 1 hay rick in Gascon		3	6
Thatching 1 hay rick in New House		3	6
Thatching 2 hay ricks in New House		4	6
Thatching 1 pea-mow in Barton		3	
Making and thatching 1 wheat mow		5	
Making and thatching 2 wheat mow		6	6
Making 2 wheat mows		4	6
Thatching 2 wheat mows		4	6
Making and thatching 1 wheat mow		5	0
Thatching 2 Barley-mows		5	6
Thatching 1 Oat-mow		5	
Making and thatching 1 Bean-mow		5	
Making and thatching 2 Bean-mow		4	6
Thatching 2 Mow-stadles		2	0
	4	17	6

[In July 1850 for Mr Andrews]

	£	s	d
Righting old hay		1	6
Thatching 1 wheat mow		2	0
Making 10 thousands of spars at 1/6	1	7	0
Cutting out of spar gads withies		4	6
	1	15	0[5]

Although William Garrett and his son George were the only thatchers in Trent at this time, little time was spent on the repair of house roofs. This was not because they were incapable of house thatching or because the local farmhouses were not thatched but because farmers did not feel it necessary to create a picturesque roof, and economized for as long as possible by having the original coat of thatch patched and repaired.

In 1849 William Garrett notes:

> *February 1st*   Work begun on Wm. Brooks House
> *February 14th*   Work begun on John Brooks House
> *5 thousand of spars at 4/- per thousand*   £1
> *2 pound of twine to use on Adam Brown's house and pig sty, 1½ hundred of nails*   1/9.

By March 1849 William Garrett had returned to farm work. Magewersle graves were the pits of mangles stored for animal fodder and were covered with a rough weatherproof coat of thatch.

Thatching 2 Magewersle graves	2/6
Thatching 1 vetch mow	2/-
2 thousand long spars	10/-[6]

Long spars anchored the thin coat of thatch onto the rick and made it more difficult for gale force winds to lift the thatch; this was important for once a small section had lifted more damage would quickly follow. Another way to make an older rick weatherproof again was to attach a thin coat of thatching reed to the side. In some areas this was called 'wexing' and was considered a two-man operation.

Sparring reed against hay rick	1/-
Sparring reed against old hay in Mow Barton	3/6
2½ thousand long spars at 5/- per thousand	12/6[7]

Cider barns were once a common sight in

its shrubby branches made nutritious fodder. The stems were crushed and chopped in a chaff cutter and then mixed with other fodder crops. Pea hulm after threshing was used for fodder but it was impossible to build a large substantial pea mow.

[February 1847:]

   1 oat mow in Cove Wood   3/6

[March 1847:]

   1 rye mow   2/-
   1 vetch mow   2/6[9]

The bill for this farmer for the 1847/8 season for 20 ricks, making spars and righting ricks amounted to £5 12s 3d but 42 ricks for another farmer over the same period of time cost little more at £6 8s 1½d. Although the number of ricks was more than double they were smaller, easier to thatch and do not appear to have suffered damage from wind and rain during the winter.

The wimble was used to make the straw rope for rick thatching and can be found in museums today, but the number of men

Dorset thatcher Simon Garrett recalls using a wimble as a boy before the First World War. In 1990 he had not forgotten the art.

To make a straw rope a wimble was required. Regional variations were common and practice was essential to form a tight, even rope

who know how to use them are dwindling. Just like the spar, the wimble was known by various names including whimble, whimmer or throw-hook. It was usually a job for two men and the wimble was often home made. One man drew a handful of straw from the rick and inserted a loop into the hook of the wimble. Twisting the wimble as he retreated the other man continued to feed fresh lengths of straw into the rope to be twisted. It was a skilled job with the unpractised operator making a loose, uneven rope that would easily fall apart. The finished length was rolled around a hazel spar until it was required. When labour was cheap the farmer found it more economical to use his own straw for ropes for his ricks rather than pay the thatcher to cut long pieces of hazel to use instead. In several southern counties the wimble was not used and 'thumb-bonds' were made by twisting straw with the hands and coiling the finished rope around the wrist. In Devon, where they called them 'thummle-benes', this method was often used and making them well required practice. In Anglesey the thatcher used two wimbles fastening them into a twisted straw belt around his waist. He then walked backwards turning the handles while two assistants fed in the straw to make the bonds.

Wimbling hay bonds was often wet-weather work and dozens of completed ropes were hung from beams until required. Long ropes were required for thatching but shorter ones were used for tying trusses of hay, straw or beans. One unusual wimble with a ladder-like frame joined by an iron pin was seen in use near Crediton, Devon, before the First World War. In Cornwall a rather elaborate wimble, called a 'wink', was used, until it was realized that imported coconut-fibre rope made a good replacement and the 'wink' disappeared long before the wimble.

As many regional variations existed in the art of rick building as in house styles. In some areas conical ricks were a common

sight but in others they were hard to find. Some regions favoured certain shapes because they were traditional and a great deal of mystery and folklore had always surrounded the success or failure of the harvest. In other areas the shape, size and style of the rick was dictated by location. On exposed sites the round rick might resist storm damage because there were no corners to be lifted by gusts of wind. Some farmers liked to see their ricks neatly clipped while others considered clipping took time and 'time meant money'. To make a round rick, it was stated, a circle should be made on the ground using a string tied to a central peg; but many rick builders instinctively knew just where to place their base sheaves. As the sides could grow to a height of eight or ten feet (2.4–3 metres) the ideal was a carefully balanced structure with an outward-facing slope which ensured that the eaves overhung by as great a distance as was possible to shed water far away from the base. The skill of the rick builder showed after a few weeks. On some farms the ricks stood straight and firm right through to the spring but others showed signs of bad construction much earlier. Some farmworkers built their ricks around a central pole and still more would erect props around the sagging sides of badly constructed ricks. The finial of the round rick resembled a 'dolly' with its turned over and bound centre – not the ornate corn dolly that is sold today in craft shops. Thatching the rick to make it watertight was of prime importance and when one was finished there was always another rick waiting, if not on that farm then on a neighbouring one. There was no time for the construction of an elaborate rick ornament. As far as the thatcher was concerned preservation of the crop was a positive action giving rise to little superstition.

From 1864 to 1867 Mrs Genge of Trent was growing flax and William Garrett thatched

Ricks at Singleton, Sussex.

These four ricks generated a great deal of interest for they were built, in 1989, by traditional methods. Only after the rick had disappeared from the countryside was it realized that a part of our heritage had been lost

3 Flax Mows in Homer Lake	6/-
2 Flax Mows in Gascon	5/-
1 Flax mow in Grove	2/6
	[as well as]
1 Clover seed rick in Plot	2/-[10]

Ricks will never be called by their regional names again. In Norfolk and Cambridge a circular rick was called a cob while a long rick of hay or wheat was called a jug. Some Kentish farmers thatched their long wheat ricks right to the ground with the upright part put on last and called the 'petticoat'. The oblong rick with hipped ends was popular in southern England, thatched in a style similar to a hipped roof. Further inland large gable-ended ricks were seen. A squat or blocklike rick with a less steep pitch, a thicker coat, longer spars and hazel or withy liggers instead of a straw rope often resisted coastal gales better. In Pembrokeshire, parts of Somerset and the Lake District, where little corn was grown, the common rush was cut green just before haymaking started and fixed in place with long hazel spars. In many parts of Wales, Scotland and at Land's End and other coastal areas the thatch was weighted down by heavy stones suspended at intervals around the eaves. In Cornwall farmers used a mesh of cords and a string of stones to protect their ricks and often drove wooden pegs, instead of spars, into the thatch with a mallet.

Some farmers would raise a rolled-up waterproof sheet on long poles ready to be draped over the rick as a temporary covering if rain threatened. Thatchers knew the ricks would bring them in the bulk of their summer income but there was no way they could organize the process to save on travelling time. The farmer wanted each rick thatched as soon as it was completed and much of the profit was lost in making several journeys to each farm during the season. Rick thatching was not very profitable but it did bring the thatcher a continuous supply of work at a time when little else could be found. When the horse and cart had been replaced by the car the headlights were beamed onto the rick on several occasions when just half an hour's work in the dark would complete the thatch and ensure a return journey would not be necessary.

Although thatchers are unlikely to be asked to thatch up to 400 ricks in a season again, the rick is becoming a more common sight in some areas and many now acknowledge it is the best and easiest method of storage. On the Somerset Levels thatcher Harold Wright is fighting to preserve traditional farming methods. In 1987 he cut a ten-acre field of Huntsman wheat and built two gable-ended ricks which he thatched. Fred Wellspring of Sydling St Nicholas made a baled rick and recalls he used to thatch up to 40 ricks a year on the farm where he worked for 50 years. Although he has experimented with various storage methods he still favours the thatched rick. His spars are single hazel pegs which are laced to a twine rope. As the bales are removed the twine and spars act as weights at the rear of the rick. The complete end still looks as neat as the day it was thatched but from the exposed end the scene is more typical of the farmyard. Using binder twine instead of a straw rope economizes on spars but requires a certain knack. If twisted spars are used a ball of twine is too large to pass through the hair-pin top and is knotted to one side. Fred Wellspring believes grants for Dutch barns encouraged farmers to abandon rick building. The Dutch barn design was not a new one however, for in 1762 Timothy Lightoler published a design for a thatched Dutch barn in *The Gentleman and Farmer's Architect* which was only one of the publications that showed the latest farming fashion.

Many small family farms were struggling and there was a reluctance to invest hard-pressed capital in new farm buildings so they continued to build ricks into the 1960s. Some farmers experimented with a waterproofed paper called Sisalcraft that arrived in rolls. Few found it a satisfactory covering as it could only be used on the calmest of days and even then it tore easily. Once draped like wallpaper over the oblong ricks it had to be secured by a temporary roping of binder twine before it parachuted into the air. It was claimed that anyone could apply Sisalcraft and during the Second World War when more fields were turned over to crop production many farmers resorted to it. Thatchers like Harold Wright of Compton Dundon spent the war years in the Middle East and others became members of the Home Guard and found it hard to keep up with their regular round of work when they had just finished their night patrols. Some farmers tried to weight the Sisalcraft down with nets or ropes that were tied to railway sleepers or large pieces of wood. Others filled old metal buckets with stones and tied these on as weights but it was a common sight the next morning to find the rick uncovered and the complete covering of Sisalcraft neatly wound up at one end of the rick like a roll of carpet. However, the price of thatching reed was rising sharply and in 1954 it was said 'At three shillings a bundle it is not a cheap roofing material for rick or barn. A fairly small rick may cost £8 or £10, and a house the same size £20 to £30 for yelms [yealms] alone if a waterproof coating is to be obtained!'.

The thatch-making machine rarely produced a regular coat of thatch and today only a few examples survive. One can sometimes be seen working at annual events such as 'Yesterday's Farming' or 'The Great Dorset Steam Fair'. The idea was first launched in 1890 but did not prove popular. Firms such as J.W. Titt of Woodcock Iron Works in Warminster, Wiltshire, advertised the sale of such machines 'for covering corn and hay stacks, mangel wurtzel, sheep folds, etc.'. It was claimed the machine could produce '1,500 feet per hour'. Advantages were numerous, they claimed; 'stack cloths can be dispensed with. Thatch can be made in winter. It can be used more than once.' The £30 cost of the machine was supposed

A baled rick at Sydling St Nicholas, Dorset.

Bales can be ricked and thatched and a few modern farmers are returning to such storage methods

The Ring, Briantspuddle, Dorset.
This model dairy farm was built in the twentieth century for Sir Ernest Debenham's estate, where he insisted every roof should be thatched

to be but a small investment although three men were usually needed to make the thatch, and rarely at half of the rate the makers claimed in field conditions. More machines were produced during the Second World War when Land Girls produced temporary rick coverings at a time when thatchers were hard to find but as soon as conditions returned to normal most thatch-making machines were rapidly retired in favour of the thatcher's craft.

'The Ring' was a popular name for many buildings. The circular design has been significant throughout history although advocates of the 'Model Farm' claimed a circular yard meant the labourer could not find a corner to hide in! At Briantspuddle 'The Ring' was built in 1919 as the first of a series of model dairy farms on Sir Ernest Debenham's estate. The whole is a large semi-circle facing a central green which still contains the walnut trees Sir Ernest Debenham planted 70 years ago. Brick-trimmed turrets link the two-storey end cottages with attics to the single-storey central sections. Although the roof and turrets were thatched to match the rest of his estate the walls were of experimental large concrete blocks made from local gravel which were unusual at that time. Halsey Ricardo, in conjunction with Sir Ernest Debenham and thatcher John Fooks, were responsible for the total concept. However Sir Ernest's wish to stem the flow of farmworkers drifting to the towns was not successful and today the farm has been divided into two privately owned cottages.

An even later model farm designed by Maurice Chesterton was built at Codicote, Hertfordshire in 1927, with a circular courtyard. The thatched farm has an elaborately designed entrance arch and a silo disguised as a thatched lighthouse. Between these two dates 'The Ring' at Leweston Manor was being thatched by Dorset thatchers Simon and Archie Garrett for months at a time between more pressing work. Designed as a covered exercise yard for hunters on the outside and with wagon, cart and implement storage bays around the inner circle, which was itself reached through an archway, it was large enough to appear on the Ordnance Survey map. The wall was stone and the roof of the exercise ring was supported on wooden poles, reminiscent of earlier ornate designs, with a sufficient span for two horses to be exercised side by side. Combed wheat reed was needed in such large quantities that the thatchers bought materials from many farmers who delivered it to the site. Over 30 tons was needed but after 20 years escalating costs made the roof too expensive to maintain. Today a bungalow stands within the walls which has kept the name of 'The Ring'.

A circular cattle shed with a thatched roof was added to Sir Thomas Gascoigne's Home Farm at Parlington, Yorkshire in 1803 at a cost of £51 10s 3d but, again, only the shell remains today.

Few model farms were thatched, for the farmers were seeking the ideal layout but incorporating all of the latest ideas. In 1812 H.E. Strickland wrote in his 'General view of the Agriculture of the East Riding of Yorkshire for the Board of Agriculture': 'But the folly even of an overbuilt farmhouse is surpassed by that of an ornamental one. What, indeed, can be so absurd and devoid of taste as a Gothicised farmhouse, or castellated cottage?' (but, he added, there were few examples).

The term 'model farm' appears to be Victorian. Many of the 'Home Farms' are referred to as model farms but few have kept to their original design and now sport later extensions that are not in keeping; some have disappeared altogether. As early as the eighteenth century purpose-built farms began to appear that showed no regard for the vernacular but, for the first time, drew their designs from architectural plans.

William Cobbett disapproved of model farms and considered large tenanted farms represented the ruin of the old yeoman class. He was right in some ways, for many model farms were not practical and proved excessively expensive to build and operate. Many landowners were tempted to follow the great agricultural improvers of their day and often followed the lead of 'Farmer George' (King George III) himself. If not, there were 30 books published on farms and rural buildings between 1800 and 1837 and a further eight during Queen Victoria's reign. Pattern books were widely read and some had reached more than four editions before 1840.

Other landowners settled for a model dairy, often as a present for the wife who had everything and plenty of time to take part in rustic pursuits. It was agreed by all that the dairy should be sited in the shade of overhanging branches a short distance from the house, but it was important that it could easily be seen by visitors. The interior was often lavishly finished with the most beautiful tile surrounds, marble work surfaces and a central fountain.

The dairy in the grounds of Blaise Castle Estate, just north of Bristol, met all of the

John Nash's thatched dairy, Blaise Castle, Bristol.

Thatch is the ideal insulator for the model dairy, providing warmth in winter yet remaining cool in summer

criteria of the day. It was clearly visible from the new conservatory that had been added at the rear of the house and nestled in a dip surrounded by a cluster of trees. The narrow verandah end surmounted by an eyebrow window is all that is visible from the house and makes the whole building appear far smaller than it actually is. No doubt the dairy was a cool retreat from the summer heat, especially if it had a thatched roof like this one. Others tried building with cavity walls to try to maintain what was considered the ideal temperature of 50°F (10°C).

It seems likely that Blaise Hamlet dairy was built in 1804 for John Harford's accounts for that year include 'Pd. for 12 dozn. of helm for thatching new Dairy at 14/- a dozn. £8.8.0.' which was a great deal of money at this time. The design is attributed to John Nash, assisted by George Repton and possibly by his brother John. John Harford's dairy was not the first of its kind. A thatched rustic dairy was added to one of the Earl of Strathmore's new farms at Bridge End. Philip Yorke's dairy at Hamels, Hertfordshire was built much earlier, in 1787, to a primitive hut design by Sir John

Soane, and was a present to his wife on their first wedding anniversary. Lady Spencer assisted Henry Holland with the design of the dairy at Althorp. Other dairies were built a little later. A rustic dairy with a thatched roof was built for the second Duke of Northumberland soon after 1830 at Alnwick Castle and the only decorative building on the Scottish estates of the ninth and tenth Earls of Strathmore was the dairy with a verandah and pretty thatched roof.

King George III was equally enthusiastic about the latest designs for farms and dairies but some of the buildings have been demolished and many were rebuilt by Prince Albert. At Frogmore, one of the royal residences, a dairy was built in about 1790 but it was later demolished and a bailiff's house built there to a neo-classical design, since altered. Norfolk Farm was built between 1791 and 1792 in the Great Park, and Flemish Farm, which also included a swineherd's cottage, was added during the next two years but has since been demolished as has the Bagshot poultry yard. The farms in the park were the joint work of

Catherington treadwheel, formerly in Hampshire and now at the Weald and Downland Open Air Museum, Sussex.

The combination of wattle and thatch on the farm forms the link between the farmer, the thatcher and the hurdle/spar maker

Stembridge tower mill, High Ham, Somerset.

The thatched cap of this tower mill is the sole surviving example of its kind and is now protected by the National Trust

Nathaniel Kent and the King himself. The buildings were of thatch, timber and brick and most incorporated older salvaged materials.

A thatched wattle shelter is an unusual survivor of what might once have been a common building. At Catherington in Hampshire a well was reputed to be over 300 feet (91 metres) deep and the bucket would have taken a long time to raise to the surface, so a shelter would have been appreciated. Here the skills of the thatcher, hurdlemaker, sparmaker and the farmer, who probably produced both the reed and the coppice wood, come together. The tread-wheel building is believed to date from the early seventeenth century and was fortunately saved by the Weald and Downland Open Air Museum when it became obsolete. Many other interesting farm buildings from which much knowledge could have been gained have not been as fortunate. The structure was functional and therefore simple. It is easy to see how numerous other shelters with thatched roofs have probably disappeared without trace.

When the farmer had harvested his crop and the threshed wheat had been ricked there was only one thing left to do. The grain required for flour had to be milled. Before the very white flour produced by the roller mill was demanded by all workers, the farmer would have sought the nearest miller. Stembridge tower mill ceased work in 1910 and owes its preservation to the National Trust who acquired it in 1969. The thatched gable-shaped cap is now unique in England and another unusual feature is the fireplace set in the lowest floor wall with a flue that runs up to just below the thatched cap. The name of thatcher Ernest Fisher of Pitney Hill is one of many names carved in the mill.

Pibsbury windmill near Langport is thought to have been the tallest Somerset windmill and also had a thatched cap. During the last 20 years of its working life the cap was covered in wood and felt, after the thatch was torn off during a gale. The mill worked until at least 1897 and part of the tower collapsed following a gale in April 1915.

The thatcher was only useful to the farmer as long as it suited the latter's farming methods and building styles. As soon as the farmer adopted new methods change crept through the whole of the farm and some thatchers sought to specialize in house thatching whilst others became thatchers of estate properties. Old traditions were slow to die out in some southern counties, especially in areas where small mixed farms were common, and here the thatcher found a steady supply of work until recent years. After a break of a decade there appears to be a closer bond developing between the thatcher and the farmer. As more farmers are looking for alternative uses for their land some, like Michael Davies of Woodbridge Farm, have chosen to set aside an annual acreage for the growth of thatching reed, although few have yet investigated the possibilities of producing organic marsh reed in suitable areas.

6

Cottage orné

What seems picturesque and ornate to some eyes may appear completely incomprehensible and unnecessary to others. The quest for different designs to adorn the countryside, and especially the large estates, started from the middle of the eighteenth century. No longer was practical design appreciated and its ability to blend into its surroundings considered aesthetic. The impractical became the desirable. Designs were published in large numbers for minute lodges, round-houses, summerhouses and follies. Over a hundred pattern books appeared in quick succession. Little thought was given to the interiors, and cottages designed to hold a gatekeeper's family would often contain just one small room with beds that doubled as window seats during the day.

Although these new designs produced fresh work for the thatcher he would have found it hard to appreciate them. The Master Thatcher had been an independent craftsman for centuries and had worked hard to provide his (often large) family with adequate living accommodation, land to be self-sufficient and the luxury of an orchard to produce his cider. He kept his own horse, cart, thatching tools and agricultural

implements and often stored a cider press in an outbuilding. The new, fashionable designs were too small to provide him with an income that could maintain this lifestyle. The conical structure had previously been used only on the rick and yet now the thatcher was expected to interpret the same skills on a house, little larger than the staddle the rick was built on. The finished article was supposed to please the eye but in quite a different way. The more rustic the interpretation the more acceptable the design seemed to be, and the straight lines that had ensured a weatherproof finish were scorned. The smaller the lodge, the larger the park appeared to be, from a distance, and these factors were considered of prime importance. The fact that the living accommodation was quite inadequate for a large family no longer seemed to matter, and little account was taken of the social improvers who specified that two, if not three, bedrooms were essential.

As the price of wheat rose during the French wars the landed gentry, predictably, decided thatch was no longer to be scorned, and they sought to use what they had previously considered the poor man's roofing material. Despite the rusticity

Plague Cottage, Stratton, Dorset, 1989.

The future of this small lodge was uncertain until recently, for it meets none of the present building regulations and has been empty for 30 years. However, plans to incorporate it as a study bedroom, forming part of a two-storey extension have just been announced. Despite the present mood favouring restoration, some dwellings will still be lost; not all will be as fortunate as Plague Cottage (which does not appear to have had any connection with infectious diseases)

desired, only experienced thatchers were invited to undertake the work; the final effect might look rough but the landowner also wanted to appreciate his follies for some years to come. Rick thatching with a thin coat of thatch sparred deeply into the undercoat was not exactly what he had in mind. Agricultural thatchers that only circulated between the farms in one village could not compete for this new work. Some did not have the experience and many did

not have the transport, ladders or necessary tools, having relied on the farmers to provide them with what was required for the job.

Even the smallest householder contemplated the addition of a summerhouse, porch or verandah to his property; hardly anyone was left out.

The cottage orné at its best could be seen near Exmouth, Devon in 1795 when 'A-la-Ronde' was thatched for two much travelled

121

The Lodge, Stanbridge, Dorset.
Stanbridge Lodge, built in 1809, was re-thatched in the 1970s but using combed wheat reed to replace its former long-straw style

ladies, the Misses Parminter, but despite its name it was hexagonal. The original thatched design was inspired by San Vitale at Ravenna and at a later date, pursuing Victorian arts and crafts, the ladies whimsically decorated the upper storey. Today the lantern and the diamond-shaped windows alternating with rectangular ones survive but the cottage is no longer thatched. Others have retained their thatched roofs but like 'A-la-Ronde' they were described as round-houses without being round.

Stanbridge Lodge was built in 1809 in the Allen Valley, Dorset and is a fine example of a rustic lodge. It was built close to the road, for everyone to admire as an entrance lodge to Gaunts House and until 1972 was thatched in long straw. Thatcher Victor Hiscock of Shaftesbury admitted it was the most unusual shape he had ever tackled when he spent five weeks working the

Umbrella Cottage, Lyme Regis, Dorset.

A polygonal cottage orné with a strange mixture of features

combed wheat reed into shape. 'While it looks like a beehive with its rounded roof, it is, in fact, rectangular with flattened corners.' He considered the long-straw coat had had a short life but not all thatchers would agree with him.

Those who specialize in long-straw thatch, especially in the eastern counties, claim that if properly applied and maintained it can compete with other thatching materials. This style would have suited the rustic vision of the landowner, with its flowing qualities. In 1972 a well in the garden was re-opened to wet the combed wheat reed to make it more pliable, and fortunately the decision was taken to re-cut clipped points along the eaves thus preserving the most unusual feature of this building.

By this time thatchers' tools were in short supply. Roberts of Faringdon were pleased to inform a thatcher in 1982 that 'we have bought up the remaining stock of shearing hooks and eaves hooks made by the late firm of Ranskil'. The cost was £8. Limited supplies of spar hooks and shearing hooks had also been obtained from Morris and Son of Dunsford, Devon and the price of these was £27.50.

Umbrella Cottage at Lyme Regis is another fine example of the bee-skep roof shape with points. Originally a toll house built in about 1810, it faces the Sidmouth road and has a most unusual roof. A more sophisticated thatching style was required to create the sleek, tightly compacted shape. The cottage appears round but is in fact polygonal.

Other cottages were true round-houses with furniture designed to fit the curve of the internal walls and thus make maximum use of the restricted space. To complete a weatherproof roof was not an easy task for the thatcher. It was difficult to add the final courses of reed as the circumference narrowed. Often the chimney poking through the apex of the roof created a

problem and a large lead apron was necessary to make a watertight seal.

The round-house on the approach drive from Nether Compton to Compton House is one of the few that is not visible from the road. Nestling beneath woods that contained the sparmaker's coppice as well as the keeper's cottage it was attractive, but not extreme in design. By the outbreak of the Second World War the importance of maintaining the picturesque had waned and the mood of the estate labourers had changed. No longer were families willing to live in such cramped and isolated accommodation and this cottage housed an evacuated family during the war. Until 1970 it remained empty but was then sympathetically extended so that the original concept of the round-house remains, and an unobtrusive extension made the cottage desirable as family accommodation.

To find five round-houses in one village points to a single family instigating their construction which must have provided one or two of Cornwall's very few thatchers with much-needed work between 1805 and 1811. Thatch in Cornwall had been more widespread but not on decorative lines. In 1602 Richard Carew described the older cottages of Cornwall as being 'walles of earth, low thatched roofes, few partitions, no planchings or glasse windows, and scarcely any chimnies'.[1] By 1700 Fiennes saw little change, describing 'poor cottages like barns' at Lands End 'much like those in Scotland'.[2]

The round-house, Over Compton, Dorset.

The true round-house is difficult to find. The thatcher often used a large lead apron to make a waterproof junction at the central chimney pot

Little more than a century later the philanthropist, the Rev. Jeremiah Trist, instigated the building of the round-houses at Veryan at a cost of £42 per house. The builder was Hugh Rowe of Lostwithiel, who would have been amazed at the 1988 market price of £125,000 for one of these cob-walled, thatched-roofed cottages. Jeremiah Trist and his son, the Rev. Samuel Trist, were both concerned about the lack of accommodation for labourers in the area but alternative local legends are numerous and often preferred. Trist had visited Africa and no doubt took his original design from the huts he had seen. A design was adapted for the Veryan houses from a plan for a circular bungalow published in Worgan's Agricultural Survey, which Trist himself had helped compile. Variations on the original design for a bedroom, pantry, woodcorner, central stove and chimney venting through the apex of the roof, exist in the four thatched cottages, with only the one roofed in slate constructed to the original design. Two pairs of round-houses stand on the entrance roads to the village and it seems unlikely that Trist really wanted them built to provide a home for each of his daughters. The pairs do appear to guard the entrances to the village and are surmounted by crosses, but whether built to allay villagers' fears about Satan, by providing round-houses with no corners for him to hide in, or just to provide more houses will probably never be known. A school for girls at Veryan built for Trist followed another of the designs in the Worgan survey, which adapted a plan for a steward's house to an oval, single-storey design with a thatched roof, and a similar design has been used for a thatched bungalow near Truro.

Designs varied according to the whims of the individual and not every landowner built cottages. Great pleasure was taken in the creation of ruined towers, monasteries, grottos and castellated follies. The thatched convent in the woods at Stourhead was built before 1770 and contrasts with King Alfred's tower sited on a nearby hill-top. Forty years earlier, the architect William Kent had designed a ruined hermitage for Queen Caroline in Richmond Gardens, with trees sprouting through the roof. In 1735 he added another folly called Merlin's Cave and this was thatched. In 1753 naturalizing began of the formal garden at Halswell near Bridgwater, Somerset, created by Sir Charles Kemeys Tynte who was a friend of Henry Hoare of Stourhead. Tynte and his architect friend Thomas Prowse both subscribed to Wright's *Book of Arbours* which was published in 1755 and his designs have many similarities to Wright's, with Halswell's thatched Druids' Temple almost identical to one of the engravings. Arthur Young in his 'Tour through the East of England' in 1771 described Halswell and the moods created by the various settings. The walk veered through scenes of gloom and confinement to open, airy, cheerful glimpses across the estate to the surrounding countryside. Today the grottos, temples and rotundas are being restored, but out of the twelve one is missing – the thatched temple that was demolished in the 1950s when few saw a future for thatch.

By the turn of the century thoughts had returned to the design of cottages. Some were to be plain rural cottages but most were to have an element of the picturesque and others carried cottage orné to the extreme. Not everyone was blind to the provision of the 'model cottage' at the expense of housing for the poor. In 1865 the system of 'close' parishes, whereby landlords could restrict numbers and so reduce the burden of poor rates on the parishioners was investigated in Bedfordshire by Dr R. Hunter who was employed by the Privy Council. The neatness he found in some villages had been created at the expense of the original inhabitants who had been forced into squalid conditions elsewhere.

One of five round-houses at Veryan, Cornwall.

Five round-houses were built here between 1805 and 1811. The total cost was £42 each, of which perhaps less than £4 would have been paid to the thatcher

127

One house called Richardson's could hardly be matched in England for original meanness and present badness of condition. Its plaster walls leaned and bulged very like a lady's dress in a curtsey. [One gable end was convex, the other concave, and one supported the chimney which was] *a curved tube of clay and wood resembling an elephant's trunk. A long stick served as a prop to prevent the chimney from falling.*[3]

[Close by Dr Hunter discovered] *two of the most ridiculous new model cottages* [he had ever seen and considered the money wasted on these could have provided a third, practical cottage that would have made the hovel no longer necessary to] *disgrace the country.*[4]

Dr Hunter was no doubt outraged by Joseph Gandy's designs but delighted that none of them were constructed, or so it appears. Architect Joseph Gandy published a book in 1805 entitled *Designs for cottages, cottage farms and other rural buildings including entrance gates and lodges*, in an attempt to carve himself a reputation by cashing in on the whims of the owners of large estates. He gave no thought to the privacy, moral standards or comfort of the inhabitants he was suggesting should be incarcerated in a circular room of less than nine feet (three metres) in diameter. He boldly stated that designs 'which are regular may be changed into the picturesque' and he was seeking 'simplicity and variety . . . both in the

Goathill Lodge, Goathill, Dorset.

Goathill Lodge has an undulating roof that tried the thatcher's skills to the fullest extent, as he laboured to produce the flow necessary to form a rounded and not an angular shape

Middle Lodge, Sherborne Park, Dorset.

Middle Lodge is almost concealed in the woods of Sherborne Park and is not lived in today although its roof is carefully maintained. Its shutters are opened for riding parties and no better stopping place could be found for lunch than in the beautiful park setting

greatest and smallest works', seeking 'a more extended idea of taste, even in buildings of the lowest class'. Gandy was not alone in his ideas but he carried them to the extreme and in many of his designs that started from around £50 to build he allowed more room for doves, poultry and pigs than for the family. Conical lodges on either side of entrance gates fortunately remained a dream. He pictured them thatched from ground level, built onto banded metal frames with a chimney in the apex of the roof, without a thought to the fire hazard

this would have created and the easy access for vermin chewing their way through walls of thatch.

Rustic pillars to support the weighty overhangs of verandahs were the norm, with some owners selecting naturally distorted pieces of wood. Gandy specified pillars should 'in all cases consist of young trees cut to size, and the bark left on'. Some landowners kept an eye to the picturesque without abandoning the more practical aspects of housing a family. Pleasing designs such as Goathill Lodge, an entrance lodge to

129

Sherborne Castle Estate, fulfilled both the desires of the landowner and the needs of the tenant.

The calculated length of the timbers formed the roof pattern for the thatcher to follow but it was his skill that created the rolling curvaceous coat in combed wheat reed. There were problems, for it was almost impossible to make a weathertight finish at the ridge where three large chimneypots protruded through the thatch. Several return visits have been necessary over the years just because the original design had not given enough thought to this problem. Goathill Lodge provided a two-bedroomed home for an estate woodsman whose job included keeping the woodland walks clear. His wife acted as gatekeeper when visitors or gentry from the house wished to pass by.

Often a park was adorned with a central lodge just visible between the trees, and not many years after John Nash's thatched Royal Lodge was built in Windsor Great Park the Digby family at Sherborne built Middle Lodge, on less ornate lines and with spacious accommodation.

The 'model' cottage was not always picturesque but rustic cottages were usually constructed with this in mind. Cottages, and sometimes whole villages, were built on these principles throughout the nineteenth century and a few in the first quarter of the twentieth century. Milton Abbas, Dorset, was completed by 1789 to replace a decaying market town that lay adjacent to the landowner's house and shows no individual characteristics in the 40 cob and thatched cottages. Furthermore, they could not have proved sufficient to rehouse the town's remaining population and there was no genuine desire to improve conditions for the inhabitants. The cottages stand like a regiment of soldiers, outwardly pleasing to the casual glance of the passing carriage occupant, but behind the walls three and sometimes four families were squashed into each cottage. Once the new work was

completed there would be no need of the thatcher's services until new ridges were required after about seven years.

Other landowners showed a genuine desire to create something pleasing and comfortable for their retired estate workers. In 1810 John Harford, a banker and the owner of Blaise Castle Estate, near Bristol, took an interest in the Picturesque Movement. His 'model' village was built the following year at Henbury and is one of the best surviving examples of combining the picturesque cottage with a genuine desire to house estate pensioners in comfort. Contrived rusticity was popular in the early nineteenth century but is not carried to the extreme at Blaise Hamlet. Here, variety of detail and a mixture of styles with rustic pole verandahs and the occasional bark-coated timber support prove both attractive and practical. The tall Tudor chimneys would have been visible from John Harford's house as a pleasing reminder of what he had achieved. His son pays tribute to this on an inscription on the village pump.

The present owner gratefully records testimony of filial affection [for] *this act of his benevolent parent.*

The cottages, designed by John Nash and G.S. Repton, were grouped around a contrived village green, complete with a central sundial and pump. Even today the peace and tranquillity he visualized can be appreciated, despite the busy road that passes nearby. Out of one double cottage and eight detached cottages, three are thatched, and although they differ in detail they are of similar size and care has been taken to position them to ensure a degree of privacy for each tenant. The story that the entrance doors were placed so that the occupants could not idly gossip seems most unfair, for on close examination of the site it is apparent that if John Harford wanted to house ten families of pensionable age he would have had to position them in such a

Blaise Hamlet, Bristol.

Circular Cottage is one of three cottages at Blaise Hamlet that were thatched. The National Trust had Jasmine Cottage re-thatched in 1973, and in 1974 restored Oak Cottage to its original design with a thatched roof

way, or sacrifice one dwelling; all of them had two bedrooms, a kitchen and scullery. On the contrary, pleasant conversation under the verandahs was encouraged by the provision of seats at some cottages with everyone able to exchange a few words across the green.

Another pleasant hamlet was created in 1828 at Selworthy in Somerset where thatched cottages were grouped around a pasture with access from a lane. The site, with good views to Dunkery Beacon on Exmoor to the south and sheltered by Selworthy Beacon to the north, was chosen by Thomas Dyke Acland, tenth Baronet Holnicote, to house retired workers from the family estate. His design was probably influenced by P.F. Robinson's *Rural Architecture* published in 1823, a well-thumbed copy of which was found in his library. Built in the vernacular style of colourwashed cob walls topped by thatch, these cottages blended into their surroundings. However, some thatched hamlets were not built until the early years of the twentieth century.

Thatch enthusiast Sir Ernest Debenham modelled his hamlet, Bladen Valley in South Dorset, on the lines of Milton Abbas, according to thatchers John and Alan Fooks who thatched all of the houses on the Debenham Estate. Others claim similarities with Blaise Hamlet which seems less likely. The number of individual styles, generously

131

Bladen Valley, Briantspuddle, Dorset.

Bladen Valley was not spoilt by the building of a new hamlet, which also provided work for the Fooks family of thatchers on a wide variety of roof shapes. The war memorial at the entrance is said to be the most beautiful in England

The Summerhouse, Sherborne Castle, Dorset.

This summerhouse was thatched with Scottish heather in 1910. Today the roof is of combed wheat reed but no less attractive

spaced and with ample accommodation, drew praise from all who admired them in their picturesque and private setting. The walls are built of experimental concrete cavity blocks constructed from local gravel, made on site with a Swedish machine, and have weathered pleasantly. Only a very close inspection reveals the true date (post-1914) of these properties.

Ardeley, near Walkern in Hertfordshire, was another post-war estate village with picturesque thatched cottages around a village green and well.

As previously mentioned, model cottages were sometimes built at the expense of those who were supposed to live in them, providing them with neither comfort nor space. No-one, however, could fault the landlord's quest for the unusual when it took the form of something as harmless as a summerhouse, boathouse or rustic covering for the village well. Extra work for the thatcher was provided only at the cost to the purse of the estate owner.

After the railway network was completed it was easier to transport new thatching materials to areas where they had not been used before. A lakeside summerhouse at

Sherborne Castle gave pleasing views of the Park and was constructed in 1910 of local stone and thatched with Scottish heather. Heather was very much in vogue at this time and produced a long-lasting thatch that darkened almost to black as it weathered. By 1983 thatch was making a great revival and the summerhouse was rebuilt on its original site with new roof timbers, and thatched in combed wheat reed by the son of the thatcher who had applied the original heather over 70 years before. This time Simon Garrett used traditional West Country methods, tying on the base coat and then sparring into place the top coat – of almost a ton of combed wheat reed – but he recalled how, as a young boy six years old, he had travelled in the high-sprung thatcher's cart to help cut the withy bonds that bound the square bales of heather and then trimmed the long stems for his father. His reward had been a trip on the lake in the dredger that was deepening the silted bed at the time. The heather had been transported from Uig in the Hebrides and after being taken to the mainland was put aboard a train that finally arrived at Sherborne railway station. Estate wagons then brought the bales to the lakeside. Archie Garrett passed the thatching needle backwards and forwards to his assistant Simon Hunt, who threaded it around the battens before passing it back to the outside. This was a much more pleasant task for the thatcher's assistant than standing in a cottage roof-space in the dark and dust of centuries to perform the same task. This heather coat of thatch was applied by tying it onto the battens without spars, and the roof was completed with a ridge of combed wheat reed.

Heather was one of the longest lasting and most attractive thatching materials and, although less common today, is still used by at least two thatchers despite problems with maintaining a supply of materials. Just as deer nibble the growing shoots of the hazel that was intended for spars and, until recently, the coypu decimated reed beds in Norfolk, so sheep graze contentedly on the young shoots of heather. Other problems can arise in conservation areas where the mood to preserve does not allow for the practical and useful harvest of a natural resource. Providing it is not overcut, a fresh interest in the uses of heather could stimulate a deeper understanding of the need to work with nature, not against it. Abandoning certain materials to nature can mean their eventual death when the plants, trees and reed beds become stifled by undergrowth. Only careful management can maintain the correct balance and in 1989 William Tegetmeier obtained supplies of heather courtesy of the National Trust.

Previously, heather had been the poor man's roofing material, cut by cottagers who held rights on the heaths. Heather thatch could be seen in Scotland, Kent, the New Forest, and Wareham Heath in Dorset, and can still be identified by its dark springy coat applied with the flowers intact, that cannot be compacted like other varieties of thatch.

Doctor Augustus Ptolomy Colmer was an avid reader of magazines aimed at the country gentleman. His neighbours at Hendford Manor in Yeovil had a summerhouse roofed in combed wheat reed.

Little Westrow summerhouse, Holwell Drove, Dorset.

This circular summerhouse was last thatched 35 years ago. The hazel liggers that were used to fix the coat of combed wheat-reed thatch in place are now visible and the ridge has sunk below the protective coat of small-gauge wire mesh

He determined his would be covered in heather about which he had read. His medical practice stretched as far as Bradford Abbas, Dorset and West Coker in Somerset but he spent his spare time as a gentleman-farmer, and Jersey cows browsed contentedly in his garden. The only way he could fulfil his dream for his summerhouse was to order the few bales of heather he required through the Country Gentleman's Association. In due course these arrived by train and were collected from Yeovil station by the thatchers. Dorset thatchers made a round journey of ten miles (16 kilometres) with their horse and high-sprung thatchers' cart to thatch the summerhouse, but today the town's administrative offices and old police station cover the site. This coat of heather was nailed onto a wooden roof with battens, not tied on as at Sherborne Castle.

Summerhouses come in a wide variety of shapes and sizes. A circular summerhouse was originally sited near the lakeside of Westrow House, Dorset and later moved to its new site. Its attractive woodwork comprises carefully selected natural-grown timber containing knots that must have taken many hours to find. The steeply pitched roof is at an extreme angle. The present coat of thatch was attached to new roof timbers 35 years ago and the pitch has shed rainwater so well that the interior of the summerhouse roof shines as golden as the day the combed wheat reed was harvested. Birds were a problem on this roof, where they hunted for insects in the thatch (although it looked as though they were intent on vandalizing it). A coat of fine-meshed galvanized wire applied when the roof was re-ridged has prevented the problem recurring.

March 1963   Little Westrow Summerhouse
Repairs to summerhouse

and fixing wire to same	£ 4	10.	0.
1 Roll of ½" wire netting	£ 6	0.	0.
	£10	10.	0

Today the summerhouse is a haven for wildlife, and robins and wrens nest inside.

Some thatched garden buildings were not strictly summerhouses. In 1785, soon after Dr Edward Jenner was married, a clergyman friend of his built Mrs Jenner a secluded retreat in a peaceful corner of the garden of their home, The Chantry, at Berkeley in Gloucestershire. Large pieces of rustic bark cover panels of gnarled and knotted elm, and ivy stems adorn the front, curving upwards to form an arched door surround. Contorted wych elm has been used for the roof timbers inside. Shortly after Doctor Jenner's first successful vaccination, in 1796, he used the building as his surgery, where he vaccinated many local residents free of charge. He lovingly referred to the building as his 'Temple of Vaccinia' and it was re-thatched in 1988.

At about the time Blaise Hamlet was completed, *c.* 1814, John Harford, a Quaker banker of Blaise Castle House, allowed himself the luxury of a timber lodge in Blaise Woods, with walls of knots, root wood and distorted branches. A drawing exists of a grotto entitled 'The Root House' using similar materials and dated 1789 and no doubt this drawing is similar to the finished lodge.

Another unusual thatched building nestles beneath trees in the deer park at King Stag, Dorset, a great distance from the main house. This small, circular building may have been a hide or a place for picnics. The circular shape has always been popular. In 1912 an oak tree near East Claydon, Buckinghamshire had a wooden seat placed around the base of the trunk and a conical thatched roof supported by posts provided shelter from the weather. As the oak tree grew the branches were allowed to grow through the roof, which was recently re-thatched in the same style, with the older more gnarled branches protruding through the thatch.

The circular shape was often used for well

canopies too. One at East Marden, Sussex is mounted on rustic poles and makes a picturesque centrepiece for the village. It must have been appreciated by the residents while they queued with their buckets for water in the pouring rain. Another thatched well in the village of Clanfield, Hampshire, is mounted on square timbers to a design more functional than picturesque. Today, small thatched wells are springing up in cottage gardens that have never contained a well. Others stand over wells that have recently been rediscovered but have probably never had a thatched roof before.

The new picturesque movement has arrived. The most unusual thatched canopy produced by Dorset thatcher Pete Hindle in recent years covers a modern lantern. In the 1960s it was thought unusual when thatcher Simon Garrett was asked to thatch a bread oven that was fed from the exterior of the property.

Unusual thatched buildings were sometimes built by town councils to enhance public gardens. In honour of Queen Victoria's Diamond Jubilee three acres of land were given to the town of Yeovil, Somerset, by Sidney Watts, a solicitor

Thatched well, East Marden, Sussex.

The thatched canopy over the village well is supported on rustic poles and makes a picturesque central feature

The Tolpuddle Martyrs memorial shelter, Tolpuddle, Dorset.

There could not have been a more fitting roof covering than thatch for this memorial shelter, as the agricultural labourers would have been familiar with the materials used

Peppards Cottage, Burrow Bridge, Somerset.

The purpose of the thatched wall was to shed water from the porous materials used in its construction. Today it is more usual to find a wall thatched for picturesque rather than practical reasons

and also Yeovil Town Mayor for four consecutive years. The largest thatched bandstand in the country is said to have been the one built at the Sidney Gardens (as they were named in 1898) as a gift from James Bazeley Petter JP, who, with his sons, was famous for his petrol and gas engines. The bandstand measured 40 feet (12 metres) wide and was 15 feet (4.5 etres) deep. It was thatched by a Dorset thatching family of two brothers and a nephew from two different villages who worked together in order to complete the roof – made of Scottish heather – in time for the official civic opening. Rustic supports were incorporated into the front with the other sides enclosed. Concerts by Yeovil Town Band, The Salvation Army Band and countless visiting bands were performed there on a regular basis until the 30 August 1972, when it was deliberately set on fire and was never rebuilt. A shelter at

Weymouth was also of rustic woodwork under a thatched roof and faced away from the onshore winds in a small garden at the seafront. Sometimes it doubled as a bandstand. It was originally thatched in long straw; a later coat of Abbotsbury reed was allowed to decay until the shelter was demolished in the 1950s.

Some thatched shelters *have* survived. In 1934 Sir Ernest Debenham, who lived near Dorchester, in the village of Briantspuddle (where he built his model village), gave a shelter and memorial seat to the village of Tolpuddle to mark the centenary of the Tolpuddle Martyrs. It stands on the green, next to the sycamore tree beneath which the six agricultural labourers met in 1831 to form the Friendly Society of Agricultural Workers. Other shelters have lost their thatch. At Bentley in Hampshire the giant wooden book with a map and history of the village carved on it, designed by Lord

139

Aldon Lodge Folly, Yeovil, Somerset.

This modern folly is a sad memorial to the cottage at Nine Springs, Somerset that was allowed to decay

Baden-Powell, founder of the scout movement, was originally protected by a long-straw thatched shelter on corner poles. Today, less picturesque, angular tiles have replaced the thatch.

The thatched wall was once far more common than it is today and was constructed for purely practical reasons at a time when labour and materials were cheap. Some thatched caps that once shed the rain from the foundations of porous walls have been replaced by tiles and others have been left to decay. Today the thatched wall is appreciated for its picturesque qualities and

modern ones are constructed where a cap of thatch is not actually needed. One thatched wall that enhances a property, forming a link between the dwelling house and thatched garage, is at Peppards Cottage, on the Somerset Levels.

An appreciation of thatch has led to a revival of interest in the material and its possibilities. One modern folly has been built in a garden in Somerset, as a nostalgic reconstruction of a childhood memory. The full-size cottage originally stood at Nine Springs, Somerset where, inaccessible and isolated, it was allowed to decay. The miniature has similarities with Queen Charlotte's thatched summerhouse, built in the Royal Botanic Gardens in 1772, that set the style for the thatched cottage orné. It is a sad reminder of what has been lost in recent years.

Thatched churches were once so common that they would have aroused little interest. Even today there are several hundred fine examples. Many survive in Norfolk and Suffolk, thatched mainly in Norfolk reed, and others can be found in the south and eastern counties and on the Isle of Wight. Proposals to re-roof a 600-year-old Norfolk church with imported reed from Romania were fortunately squashed, although the case helped to highlight the present shortage of Norfolk reed.

To find a modern church with a thatched roof is unusual. A most unlikely industrial village was built by F.H. Crittall in the late 1920s, in a mixture of styles for his employees at his metal-window factory in Essex. Silver End was a mixture of neo-Georgian and flat-roofed modern-style cottages and a thatched church.

St George's Church at Langham, Dorset, was built by the Manger family in 1921 as a

St George's Church, Langham, Dorset.

Thatched churches were once the norm but many lost their thatched roofs centuries ago. St George's is unusual in that combed wheat reed was chosen for its roof in the twentieth century

Woodsford Castle, Dorset.

Woodsford Castle is, more accurately, a fortified house and a rare survivor from the days of Edward III. Thatch was not its original roof covering, but in 1978 its importance was realized by the Landmark Trust, who decided to have its massive roof re-thatched

memorial to those who lost their lives in the First World War, and for the use of their estate workers. It was designed by E. Ponting in simple Arts and Crafts Gothic and was built over the grave of Alfred Manger, who unfortunately did not live to see his plans carried out. It is still maintained by the Manger family and services are held there at festival times, especially the Royal British Legion Festival of Remembrance.

Some thatched properties are unusual only in being the sole survivors of a particular type of building. Large expanses of thatch are not uncommon, and thatched tithe barns can be high for the thatcher to tackle; but Woodsford Castle in Dorset is one of the most unusual thatched buildings in the country. Building work started in around 1335 when William de Whitefield, Lord of Woodsford, was granted a 'licence to crenellate'. Not only does his castle reach three storeys high, requiring a special ladder to be kept at the castle to enable the thatchers to reach the roof, but it was not originally thatched. Thatch replaced a leaking lead roof several centuries ago. A modern thatcher, Len Paul of Broadmayne, found it was the largest and highest roof he had ever tackled and at the time it was constructed thatchers did not work from scaffold. In 1630 Coker found 'Te castell is nowe almost ruinated' when he surveyed the county of Dorset. Although restoration work took place in about 1850 under the supervision of local architect John Hicks with help from the author Thomas Hardy, it had gathered several agricultural lean-to buildings against its walls and by 1906 Sir Frederick Treves described it as 'an unkempt farmhouse'.

Woodsford Castle was acquired by the Landmark Trust in 1978, the first time in 600 years that it had changed hands other than by inheritance. The Trust was founded *c.* 1965, and its purpose is to save small historic buildings and follies which may be overlooked by larger organizations.

Many of the picturesque and unusual creations that had seemed so important until the 1870s, and others that were created by late enthusiasts up until the First World War, have disappeared without trace and often have not been recorded. Some of the remainder seem to be suffering still and, although preserved for the present, the time will come when the owner must ask if the cost of repair still seems worthwhile. When that time comes, few of the craftsmen who interpreted these unusual designs so successfully and kept them repaired over the years will be available to re-thatch them in their vernacular style. Coarse-stemmed imported reed might preserve the thatch, but it cannot recreate the flowing lines of locally grown materials.

Cottage orné brought no real hope of a secure future for the thatcher. The height of the buildings was never excessive but the estate owners often wanted their latest whims thatched at once, with no regard to the thatcher's calendar. One small cottage could create more problems than profit, especially if the thatcher felt obliged to give priority to this work, for someone who could well be his landlord.

7

Thatcher - the man

The thatcher himself is not well documented. His independence has contributed to the lack of surviving evidence on his way of life. Manorial Court rolls record his materials and tools, but not his name and we shall never know how he spent his spare time.

In 1562 a general system of employment was implemented such that apprentices had to serve seven years and come from landless families to be trained by 'wheelwrights, ploughwrights, carpenters, millwrights, masons, plasterers, sawyers, limeburners, brickmakers and bricklayers, tilers, slaters, tile makers, linen weavers, coopers, earthen potters, thatchers and shinglers'.[1]

These apprentices became the founder members of the thatching families who survive in small numbers today. Only the most unusual stories have been remembered and much of the folklore of the thatcher has been lost for ever. Clues to the pursuits of previous generations of thatchers can often be found in the hay tallets and stables of those families who still live on the original family smallholding. A general pattern has emerged from interviewing many of the older craftsmen and it seems likely that similar lifestyles were enjoyed by other

thatching families. One Dorset thatching family, the Garretts, has a verbal folklore as well as a photographic record and a great deal of documentary evidence has survived to substantiate their claims. Fortunately, other thatching families are realizing the importance of recording their history and the long established Farman and Dodson thatchers of Norfolk are now recording their memoirs.

Most of the older craftsmen have a wide knowledge of country matters and a deep understanding and love of their countryside. The thatcher was a solitary man working at a height that gave him a good view of the surrounding countryside so it is not surprising that he observed the life of animals, birds and man in detail. He often showed an interest in art, music and a wide variety of other crafts too.

Before the organ and harmonium destroyed much of the community's involvement in providing the church music, craftsmen were often the instrumentalists who filled the church galleries.

The Reverend George Fort Cooper called his cartoon 'A Country Choir' in 1835, following the style of Thomas Webster's 'The Village Choir'. He was not poking fun

The choir of St Andrew's Church, Yetminster, Dorset, 1835.

'A Country Choir', drawn by the Rev. George Fort Cooper in 1835, is one of the first clues to the thatcher's social life. Thatcher Charles Brake played the clarinet in the gallery of this church

at his choristers and musicians and was well liked by his parishioners, who erected a memorial to him after his death in St Andrew's Church at Yetminster, Dorset. James Langdon, the 38-year-old schoolmaster of scientist Robert Boyle's Endowed School, is shown conducting and is seen with the singer William Patten. The musicians are: the miller William Cooper playing bassoon; flute-player Samuel Granger who was the parish clerk; plasterer and tiler William Bright Richardson playing the viol; and 43-year-old thatcher Charles Brake playing the clarinet. Tiles had already made an impact in the south and must have

been a relatively new occupation of the man who stood in the choir alongside the thatcher. The choir is made up of independent men who worked flexible hours and may have been able to earn the spare cash to purchase their instruments if they were not owned by the parish.

Other thatchers played in village bands. At Thornford, Archie Garrett taught himself to play the accordion and a penny brass whistle for his own amusement and one evening a week played the kettle drum with the Drum and Fife Band at the Parish Barn. Archie's sisters, Kate and Eva, played the piano. When Kate married gamekeeper

145

Steve Lane his working life took them to various small, keeper's cottages, but room was always found for her piano. Caleb Ryall's milk float was borrowed for each move and the first thing to arrive was always Kate's piano.

Thatcher Fred Wright always brought his accordion on the annual Master Thatchers Association outing to accompany the many well-known songs enjoyed on the coach trip home. Even today, one thatcher at Weymouth is a folk singer and has recently made a record.

The Huguenot Le Fevre family fled from France to England in the early eighteenth century with little bar their skill as hand-loom weavers, but soon established their own cottage industry in Dorset. Despite the threat from steam-powered mills their craft lingered on, but the prices were falling and weavers' sons were often forced to work as agricultural labourers. The Le Fevres lost not only their craft, but also their name, which the Dorset people found impossible to pronounce. They became the Feavers but their proud memories did not die. When Jane, who had received no formal education, fell in love with a thatcher, her parents were reluctant to give permission for them to marry. They considered that impoverished weavers who had become agricultural labourers ranked above the village thatcher, who had in fact received more education, and had a skill and sufficient money to support a wife.

When Jane married Samuel, in 1856, her life was reasonably comfortable. Their cottage was large, with a stable for their horse, a cart shed, an orchard and a paddock. Samuel became well known for his cider. He used the mobile cider mill that toured the villages in the autumn, but owned a cider press and made the cheese by mixing the crushed apples with layers of hollow thatching straw. His children attended school, and one daughter became the village schoolmistress until marriage took her to Kent.

Perhaps Samuel knew 'The Thatcher's Call':

Reed, Spars, Cyder Jar,
Boy and all,
Bring me last
What I first called!

Samuel's unfortunate Uncle George was a good thatcher, but best remembered as the giant of Over Compton. As George approached his fortieth birthday he started to grow again. He and his brother William, and cousins Nathaniel and Mark, were the thatchers of the Compton Estate, and the Goodden family, who owned the estate, took an interest in his strange condition and arranged for him to consult their doctor. The story was retold a century later, in 1970, that the doctor's potion certainly stopped George growing any taller but he started to put on weight instead and eventually his huge size stopped his thatching career. He became under-keeper on the estate but died a few years later.

Fashion, furnishing and flowers filled the spare time of thatcher's daughter Eva Maud. Although her health in childhood had been poor she lived to be 102 and clearly recalled her childhood days on the family smallholding. Her mother, who had died of diabetes when Eva was nine years old, had been a fine kid-glove maker before her marriage. Her father had been a skilled thatcher, who had insisted that if more than a handful of thatch was dropped it had to be collected and inserted into a sheaf ready for use the following day.

Jane (née Feaver) and Samuel Garrett at Stallen, Nether Compton, Dorset, c. 1885.

Jane Feaver's parents were against her marriage to a thatcher and it took a great deal of persuasion before they accepted Samuel

He supplemented his income by farming his smallholding and the arable half-acre allotment strips. Although he valued education and could read and write, few knew of his skills, and true to his Romany appearance he loved horses, keeping two of his own and trading in others. He did not send his son, Archie, to school until 11 January 1879 when he was eight years old. Even at that age there were many occasions when a boy could be useful: he could fetch the horse, unload the materials, gather up the old straw and sweep up. When Archie was too small to climb a ladder and carry a bundle of reed, weighing up to 28 pounds (13 kilogrammes), he was expected to find some way of overcoming the problem – his solution was to turn the bundle sideways and push it up the ladder, balancing it on his head. On one occasion Simon William was threatened with a summons if he did not send Archie to school, and Thornford School Minute Book reads:

January 20th 1880. Standards.

Archie Garrett came back for the examination. He is very backward in his work as he has been away at work for several months.

[New weekly charges were]
Farmer's and dairymens children   4d,
Tradesmens children   2d,
Labourers children   1d[2]

Eva recalled drawing a hollow-stemmed piece of reed from a bundle to use as a straw to suck up the fresh apple juice that flowed from the cider press to a trough in the yard. Her first attempts at milking had been a disaster when the cow kicked the full pail over and Eva received a scolding from her father. The children were sent to church three times each Sunday and Eva recalled wearing a hat as wide as an umbrella. When her father reached the age of 65 he had sufficient funds to enable him to retire.

Vine Cottage itself, where Eva lived, was spacious, with a parlour, living-room and back kitchen extension complete with its own well! Roller blinds hung behind fine, lace curtains. Besides Eva's piano there was a pine cupboard made to order to fit a wall of the living-room and such refinements as a hip bath. The hip bath ended its days outside as a water butt used for soaking thatching materials!

The vine that gave the cottage its name produced hard, green grapes that were sour but made a good wine. Simon William's secret brew was a potent spirit distilled from the young tendrils of the vine.

William Garrett, a thatcher and smallholder, recorded in his day book:

9th October 1852 sold 3½ bushels of appels at 3/- per bushel.
[In 1859 he sold] *2 appel trees   10/-.*

His son, George Garrett, carried out drilling and sowing for other farmers as well and in 1884 sold

1 sack of barley	14/-
1 calf	15/-
100 coles	15/-[3]

(Coles were open-hearted cabbages.)

A camera was beyond the pocket of most people in the village but Emily May Garrett, the eldest daughter of a Dorset thatching family, purchased one and sent it home from Winchester, where she worked, for her brother Simon and sisters Freda and Ina Joan to use.

Vine Cottage, Thornford, Dorset, 1910. Thatcher Simon William Garrett at the age of 65 (and looking forward to his retirement). Seen here with his daughter, Eva Maud.

The thatcher's roof was said to be in the same state as the shoes of the cobbler's children – always the last to be repaired; the roof of Vine Cottage is shown covered in nest-holes

---

Emily May Garrett leaves her home at Vine Cottage, Thornford (*c.* 1922) for Sherborne station, accompanied by her mother Clara and brother, thatcher Simon Garrett.

Dandy performed well in the shafts of the governess cart or the thatcher's working outfit but was often reluctant to be caught

Photography was popular amongst the boys at the Winchester Preparatory School where Emily was House Matron. The money was available for film and developing costs and many photographs survive, including one of the family's white horse, 'Dandy', who behaved impeccably once caught, both in the shafts of the governess cart or the working cart, but often preferred to canter around the field first. However, he was a great improvement on the strawberry roan who could be caught at will and

stepped out prettily, but often refused to move at all, kicking the cart with his hind legs. The family often regretted that the faithful 'Polly' had become lame after being bitten by an adder. Veterinary treatment had saved her life but the wound had irretrievably weakened the leg and she was sold.

A new thatcher's high-sprung cart, such as was made by the Brister family of wheelwrights in 1910, cost £14. Clara Hunt, who married into a thatching family, recalled other forms of transport. Large mews for horses and grooms stood behind the London house where she and her sister Annie were kitchen maids. The servants were not allowed to talk to the grooms and communicated by sign language. Clara and Annie agreed to meet two of the grooms on their afternoon off but, seeing them on foot, at first did not recognize the short bandy-legged men who walked towards them. They then agreed they could not possibly be seen out with them and leapt aboard a passing horse bus. During the shooting season the staff left for the Yorkshire country house where life was even busier than in London, with 200 birds arriving in the kitchen after each day's shoot.

A few years later, *c.* 1895, both sisters were married and living with their young families in Dorset. Annie in her donkey cart would arrive at Clara's house whether she wished to or not, for the donkey knew there would be a carrot waiting for him. On the return journey to Mogers Leaze, when he sensed he was nearing home and the mood took him, he would put his ears back and gallop at high speed with Annie pulling on the reins to no avail.

There was no tax on a working cart but 7/6 (37½p) was payable annually on the governess cart. The horse needed to be shod regularly, but in later years it was often better to ride him to the next village where his new shoes were fitted immediately for 7/6 rather than visit the local blacksmith who was now more interested in the motor car.

Simon Garrett, as a boy of six in 1910, drove with his father and uncle to Sherborne and as they approached Dancing Hill, crowds lined the terrace watching the sky. The family were thatchers for Sherborne Castle Estate and drove their horse and cart into the castle grounds. After a short while the hum of new machinery filled the air and the first aeroplane Simon had seen could be seen using the railway line as a guide to bring the pilot over the castle grounds before landing by the lake. After that date Simon saw two hot-air balloons but no more aircraft until the First World War.

In 1904 there were 8,000 cars in Britain and the first one to be driven the five miles (eight kilometres) from Yeovil to Thornford reached its destination with its radiator boiling and attracted a crowd that included thatcher Archie Garrett. Twenty years later there were 474,000 cars in the country and soon afterwards the thatchers changed their form of transport, selling their horses for the good price of £25 each. The decision to change from a horse to a car was not an easy one for a thatching family with a lifetime's association with horse transport but road surfaces were deteriorating for a horse and cart, and the pace was slow. The car increased the accessible working area and there was no longer the problem of where to stable the horse. The working day could start later as the horse did not have to be fetched from the field and fed, and later groomed and fed again.

The Model T Ford was the fifth car to be owned in Thornford and cost £50 secondhand, the price including a short driving lesson. The new price would have been in the region of £110. The other cars in the village in 1926 were owned by the Rector, a farmer, the blacksmith and the wealthy Miss Gadesden, whose large car was driven by her chauffeuse. Miss Gadesden's brother still preferred a full coach and horses, complete with postilion who sounded his horn as he approached a corner.

Once started the Model T proved reliable but it was essential for the thatchers to carry a spare two-gallon (eight-litre) can of Shell petrol costing three shillings. There were few garages and the majority of the thatchers' work was in the heart of the countryside. The roads were littered with hazards such as horseshoe, donkey and ox-

Vine Cottage, Thornford, 1925. The Garrett thatchers have taken a major decision to change their mode of transport.

The Model T Ford enabled them to widen their working area. However, Archie poses at the wheel only to have his photograph taken. He was always a horseman and never learnt to drive

shoe nails, hob nails from boots and a wide variety of protective ironwork from boots and shoes. The most puzzling puncture was caused by a gramophone needle!

The thatcher using a horse and cart needed to pack the horse's nose-bag, see the cart lamps were full of oil and pack his own food before he set off to work. In early days the costrel, a small wooden cask, contained the day's cider, and the food was packed into a rush basket. The top of a cottage loaf was cut in half and packed with cheese. Whole round cheeses were bought direct from the farm since there were considerable savings to be made if the money was available to invest in bulk quantities of food.

Some men liked a whole raw onion a day too. Thatcher George Garrett of Trent always packed his meal in a rush basket. He was the last of his line to thatch for his son was killed in the First World War. Like many thatchers he practised his craft into old age. When he did not return home one

George Garrett, thatcher of Trent, Dorset, c. 1930.

Returning from work, George Garrett pauses for his photograph to be taken. His woven-rush lunch basket hangs over his shoulder

day, he was found at the base of the Mellmoth's hay rick that he had been thatching. He had died peacefully while eating his lunch in the shade. Another thatcher from Shave Cross climbed down from the roof one day and he too sat down and died. Other thatchers were disabled after falling from the roof, some died of pneumonia and many suffered from rheumatism and arthritis in old age. When working on a barn roof one thatcher had a lucky escape; unable to save himself when a timber cracked beneath him, his son was able to pull him from the gap he was slipping through. They were surprised to see a large water-tank on brick pillars beneath them and could only think it had been winched into place and the barn built around it. Those thatchers that liked their cider seemed to suffer least when falling from the roof, and would pick themselves up and start work again.

Although most thatchers did not take part in village sports, as they worked irregular (but flexible) hours, they were able to take a day off if they chose. The charabanc was not fast but there was little traffic, no roadworks or traffic lights so the average speed was reasonable. Cheddar Caves was a popular venue for outings. When the charabanc

A visit to Cheddar Caves, Somerset, *c.* 1922.

Two free tickets were won at Sherborne Carnival by thatcher's daughter Joan Garrett (*back left*). Flexible hours enabled two thatchers and two woodsmen to accompany the women on a trip to Goughs Caves at Cheddar. Unknown to them a small boy is playing marbles in the road

known as 'The Whippet' made the return trip from Weymouth, Mrs Iris Payne, the granddaughter of a shepherd and sparmaker, recalled that the passengers had to walk up steep Ridgeway Hill, pushing if necessary. The Boys' Bible Class outing to Weymouth by charabanc took place despite the fact that the thatcher's son and friends succeeded in setting the chimney alight at Glebe Cottage where they met.

The *Western Gazette* reported on 4 March 1887:

Through the kindness of Major-General Clay of Thornford, a large number of healthy young chub have recently been turned into Yeovil Angling Association's waters.

It is doubtful whether the fish ever had the opportunity to swim as far as Yeovil for the village boys heard of the General's plans and netted most of the fish the same night.

General Clay was often rowed, by thatcher Archie Garrett, in a flat-bottomed boat down the River Yeo to Smith's Bridge at Bradford Abbas, where a mooring ring can still be seen. Thatchers developed strong arm muscles and Archie Garrett won the purse of money offered by General Clay to the man who could climb the high flag pole he gave to the village.

During the two great blizzards in the nineteenth century, Archie joined snow-clearing gangs to open up the roads to Sherborne. At Sherborne Lake in 1891 the ice was thick enough to support a large crowd of spectators and a platform on which an ox was roasted.

Yeomanry volunteers were recruited soon after the First World War when patriotic feelings were running at their highest. However, regular practice sessions and compulsory annual camps interrupted the thatcher's work at his busiest time of year. Thatcher Simon Garrett joined the advance party with Sergeant Major Sparks in 1924 but others rode their horses over 20 miles (30 kilometres) to reach the camp site at

Dorset Yeomanry volunteer Simon Garrett at camp near Weymouth, Dorset, 1924.

Too young to enlist in the First World War, many young men joined the Yeomanry volunteers. The two-weeks compulsory annual camp often disrupted the thatchers' schedule at their busiest time of year.

155

Jordan Hill, Dorset where 600 horses were tethered. Their first job was to unload 130 tons of equipment from a flat-decked cruiser that had sailed from London to Weymouth harbour. The camp finished on Saturday, 26 July and the men found it impossible to pack the bell tents, marquees and equipment back into the same amount of space and the ship had to sail with some equipment fastened to the deck.

The following July, the 15-day Bulfords Field Camp was held on Salisbury Plain. Over 1,000 horses were ridden to Larkhill Corner where army blacksmiths were waiting to replace shoes lost on the long journey. Recruitment officers tried once more to persuade the local thatcher's son to enlist, for he was one of the few men who could drive a car and the army was phasing out horses.

Owning a car was an advantage and taxi work was readily available, either transporting the village cricket team or meeting passengers off the Channel Island boats.

The thatcher was clever with his hands and experimented with a wide range of crafts during his spare time. Most could make a simple straw plait and some could produce the eight-straw plait; but few made them for profit. Many of the thatchers' craft items were useful but some were highly decorative such as oriental designs in fretwork. The patterns were available in a weekly woodwork magazine but the wood often had to be salvaged from packing cases. The stable provided the workshop but it did not guard against the inquisitive nature of younger sisters. Joan Garrett tried her hand at cutting an intricate shape but broke the blade of the fretsaw!

The hay tallet above the Garretts' stable at Vine Cottage, Thornford, was a popular meeting place for school friends. A cannon was constructed from the box (bearing) from a cart wheel and gunpowder was available at all ironmongers shops. One night the cannon was used to set fire to tar barrels in the village street and on another it broke the window of a cottage. On its last outing too much powder was used but although the boy that lit the charge fell over a friend, no-one was hurt when the cannon exploded and part landed in the rectory garden after shaving a piece from an elm tree.

More peaceful pursuits were the making of flowers from hazel, willow, spindle wood or even the hard wood of the hornbeam. Hedgerow baskets could be made from hazel or willow and the smooth wood of the elder made shuttles that held the string for making nets. Nets were useful for poaching or netting birds as they flew from their nest-holes in thatched roofs, and for enclosing the cabbages that were often cooked whole. A relation of an East Coker thatcher was apprehended on a poaching trip. The long poacher's net was strong and the constable died when the net was pulled tight around his neck.

To net enough sparrows for a pie the thatcher and a boy would climb onto the roof at dusk, when most birds had returned to their nest-holes. To the thatcher, sparrow-catching was a sport which resulted in a tasty pie and an undisturbed sleep at dawn when usually the stirring birds would

---

(*Previous page*) **Craft items made by a thatching family.**

Crafts played an important part in the thatcher's spare time. Fine fretwork, hedgerow baskets, rush and straw plaits, netting needles and spacers and flowers of hornbeam, hazel and willow illustrate just a few of the skills of one thatching family

A straw bee-skep at Perry's Cider Mills Museum, Dowlish Wake, Somerset.

Although this straw bee-skep was not made by a thatcher, many were. The thatcher's son counted out the correct number of straws for his father to work with. As winter approached the thatcher made the winter 'hackle' to protect the skep

have created enough noise to wake him up, but to the labourer it was a source of income. The price paid by the Vestry for a dozen dead sparrows was two pence, increasing in many areas to four pence in 1774. The East Coker Church accounts showed '2d a piece for Jays, 2d for Woops [bullfinches], 4d for polecats'. In 1779 35 hedgehogs, 164 woops, 4 polecats, 90 jays, 11 stoats, and 866 sparrows were presented for payment. One year 109 polecats were handed in.[4] Today most thatched roofs are protected by small-gauge wire or plastic netting, and nest-holes are few. Marsh reed is too hard for the birds to peck holes in but the sedge or combed wheat ridge is usually wired for protection. In Devon, many combed wheat-reed roofs were never wired, and at Bow, Moretonhampstead and Broadhembury this tradition has been continued. Surprisingly, few nest-holes appear in the combed wheat reed in these areas but no plausible explanation has been offered as to why this should be so.

One thatcher, who also made spars and hurdles, was a natural artist. His portraits, which included Lord Roberts and Kitchener, were copied from biscuit tins and were indistinguishable from the originals.

The construction of the straw bee-skep was a time consuming but satisfying project, and could provide a useful income on wet days or for the retired thatcher and sparmaker. In rural areas the straw skep was popular until the First World War. The straw was compressed by passing it through a piece of cow's horn and each layer was bound together with split withy, bramble or hazel. Simon Hunt asked his neighbour, Archie Garrett, who had counted the straws for his father to make skeps, to make him two just before the First World War. In the winter a straw 'hackle' resembling an umbrella, was made to provide extra insulation and to shed water from the skep. The straw skep is banned in some areas today because it is thought to harbour disease, and few know how to make one. Mr Raymond Samuel Tudor of Dowlish Wake made skeps until 1973 and was President of the South West Somerset Beekeepers Association. His skeps cost £4 each, compared to £47 for a wooden hive, and he demonstrated his craft at the annual Bath and West Show, claiming that a turkey leg bone was a vital part of his equipment!

Flora Thompson observed of one old lady in her locality:

The rest of the year was devoted to her beehives. These stood in a long line beneath a hedge of flowering currant, not painted wooden houses . . . but yellow straw skips, each roofed by a red pan, weighted down by a stone.[5]

Winter hackles were not universal, for some skeps were kept permanently beneath a thatched shelter, others were covered with hessian and a few were set into bee boles – the alcoves built into stone walls especially for this purpose. The thatcher used beeswax to waterproof his twine before tar twine became available. In 1893 William Bear remarked he had found many agricultural labourers who kept a pig and some poultry, but had not found any who kept a cow and only a few who kept bees.

Straw roof ornaments are very popular today. Twenty years ago only a few thatchers chose to leave their individual mark on houses they had thatched. Various methods were tried, but few attained the skill of the late Steve Wright from the Somerset Levels, who was a thatcher until a fall from the roof damaged his back and forced him to seek an allied occupation. He finely sculpted all sorts of animals and birds but claimed it took him many attempts before he perfected the technique. Sadly, since his death in 1988 no-one has continued his craft as a full-time occupation.

Not all thatchers supplemented their income by producing craft items. At Church Knowle, thatchers Thomas Fooks aged 15

Straw roof ornaments depicting a variety of birds and displayed at Perry's Cider Mills Museum, Dowlish Wake, Somerset.

Only in recent years have roof ornaments become a common sight in most areas. Sadly, the thatcher who made these died in 1988, leaving no-one to take his place

years, Joseph Fooks aged 38, and Robert Fooks aged 27 were all convicted of smuggling and sentenced to six months' imprisonment in the Dorset County Gaol. In 1832 Owermoigne thatcher Charles Bascombe, aged 26 years, was charged with assisting in landing contraband and assaulting a customs officer. Thatcher John Garrett stole a hen coop when he was 13 in 1852 and spent a week in gaol, during which he was whipped once. In 1854 he was convicted for 'stealing barley and a bag'[6] and his father was imprisoned for six months for the same offence.

'Most of our thatchers are old now, and there is no inclination in our youths to adopt a trade, which, in exposure to bad weather and the bitter cold of winter, gives little comfort.'[7] Anthony Pearman said these words in 1953 and this trend continued for the next 20 years. In 1966 only three young thatchers were present at a social evening organized by the Dorset Master Thatchers Association. The formation of local county branches was encouraged by the Rural Industries Bureau (RIB) in 1947, who provided encouragement and advice. On occasions their legal advice was invaluable.

161

Dorset Master Thatchers Association Christmas Party, held at Piddletrenthide, 1966.

The Master Thatchers Associations provided valuable social contact for the craftsmen when their morale was at its lowest. Most of these thatchers were approaching retirement age in 1966, when few young men were interested in learning the craft

There have been very few occasions when a dispute between the thatcher and his client has resulted in the threat of legal action, except where the final bill has not been settled quickly. One thatcher borrowed a ladder hung under the eaves of a cottage to save bringing a shorter ladder of his own. Although permission had been given, the ladder had not been moved for years and when it was put back on the wall again it looked very different from how the owners remembered it. Its condition had previously deteriorated unnoticed, as layers of dust and cobwebs had accumulated. The intervention of the RIB prevented legal action but from that date the thatcher never borrowed a ladder again.

The social contact (helped by the RIB), that had previously been missing amongst the thatchers, helped at a time when many difficulties faced their craft. The Rural Development Commission, formerly the RIB and CoSira, knows of over 400 thatching organizations and estimates the number of thatchers and apprentices could today (1990) exceed 900.

The Dodson thatching team from Kings Ripton, Cambridgeshire, numbers 15. Malcolm Dodson and four of his brothers, who can claim a thatching history over four generations, head this team, which is probably the largest in the country. Four generations ago the family cut their own reeds but the marsh was later drained and ploughed. Today the Dodson team travels much further afield and has undertaken work in the Channel Islands and Scotland.

The Farman family have been thatchers in Norfolk for almost 500 years. In 1925 Arthur Farman spoke to a national newspaper at Salhouse Broad of watching the 'picturesque sight of the large, flat-bottomed boats, laden with their high load of reeds, passing down the rivers like floating haystacks, to the staithes'. Arthur Farman had thatched bungalows in Holland and France with Norfolk reed and had introduced the decorative diamonds and scallops cut into the reed coat and not just the ridge that is so sought after today. He best remembered using this style of thatch on the entrance way to York Cottage, Sandringham for the marriage of King George V. Today, the youngest member of the Farman thatchers is 38 years old and there are no more young family apprentices to carry on their long tradition.

Some thatchers gave up their craft for health reasons. Robert and Hubert Helliar had been taught to thatch by their father and grandfather, but also farmed. The whole family suffered from asthma, and their father died of the condition when Robert was ten years old. Robert thatched at Bishops Caundle and Hubert at Caundle Marsh. Both wrote an excellent copperplate and Hubert wrote poetry but was later crippled by rheumatism. Asthma, probably made worse by their continual exposure to moulds, wheat dust and grass pollens, caused them both to retire from the roof. Another brother did not thatch but went to London and helped lay the electricity cables beneath the River Thames.

By 1987 thatch was popular again. The five surviving founder members of the Dorset Master Thatchers Association were guests of honour at the Fortieth Anniversary celebrations held at Lulworth Castle Estate. The county could now boast a large number of thatchers with half of their working life

still in front of them and enough apprentices to ensure the next generation of thatchers would be there to take their place.

All over the country a similar story can be told, but especially in the south and south-east where the demand for thatch is such that a premium may be paid for the most picturesque and sound result executed in the quickest period of time. A few thatchers in Scotland carry on their family tradition but usually it is not their sole occupation. Jonathan MacDonald on the Isle of Skye is

Dorset Master Thatchers Association fortieth anniversary celebrations, Lulworth Castle, 1987.

Bill Martin, here aged 95, was the founder-chairman of the Dorset Master Thatchers Association. In 1987 he and other surviving founder members Len Paul, Simon Garrett, William Male and Ernest Goddard were guests of honour at the fortieth anniversary celebrations at Lulworth Castle, where they were joined by president Wilfrid Weld and secretary Ronald Miller

one of the few thatchers to work using rush. Peter Brugge has thatched in Scotland and the north of England where house prices are lower, and a great deal of imported marsh reed is used because no thatching materials are grown locally.

The thatcher is well known for his ready sense of humour and perhaps it is this quality that helped him through the years when the future seemed bleak. Today his humour still shines through. Thatcher Edward Coney entered his skilfully thatched float in carnivals during 1989. In 1974 Simon Garrett thatched a roof for the carnival float of the Third Sherborne Guide Pack and shortly afterwards farmer Henry Fry made two ornamental thatched ricks for his carnival float that was pulled by two oxen called Oxo and Bisto. Thatcher Ron Gosney recalls one thatcher who could not obtain a replacement soft roof for his car and thatched it instead: it became known as 'The Hedgehog'.

Two Dorset thatchers talk at Manor Farm, Thornford.

However busy the modern thatcher may be, he still finds time to talk about his craft. Pete Hindle, a first generation thatcher with 16 years experience has taken over much of the thatching area of Simon Garrett who, with 70 years experience, has recently retired and has no son to carry on his craft

Shaftesbury Carnival, Dorset, 1989.

The thatcher's sense of humour shines through as strongly today as ever before. Thatcher Edward Coney (*centre*) entered a thatched carnival float and joined in the fun of Shaftesbury Carnival

THATCHERS DO IT ON THEIR KNEES

Hopefully thatchers will always be sociable and retain a lifelong interest in their craft. Good thatchers are not necessarily born into the craft and only some are gifted with the thatcher's natural eye for what looks just right on the roof – their thatching style is unmistakable.

The number of thatchers in the country cannot be accurately assessed, as the 1951 to 1981 censuses class thatchers with roofers and glaziers. Although numbers are increasing they will never reach the number recorded in 1841 when the total for Great Britain was over 4,000. In England there were 3,517 thatchers aged over 20 years and 157 younger men. Wales declared 58 but all were over 20. Scotland had 255 men plus seven under 20 years of age and 44 thatchers were recorded on the off-shore islands. Devon had 840 thatchers, Dorset 280, Cambridgeshire 171, Hereford 73, Gloucester 69, Cornwall 57, Hertford 45, Bedford 41, Berkshire 36, Chester 18, Derby 13, Buckinghamshire 11, and Durham 3.[8]

Not all of these thatchers prospered however, for on 6 June 1841 nine thatchers were in workhouses, one was in hospital, five were in gaol and two in lunatic asylums. Few of the hundreds of sparmakers declared this as their sole occupation but in 1841 there were 32 male sparmakers and just one woman. It would be nice to think this was Thomas Hardy's character Marty South from *The Woodlanders*! Although women thatchers are far from rare today, they do not appear to have taken to sparmaking.

The thatcher's social life has always been interesting and varied; all over the country similar stories have been told but unfortunately few have been recorded.

8

Help at hand

Today's thatch owners are very different from those who went before, for thatch is their choice of roofing material rather than having been dictated by necessity. A wealth of information is available on materials, methods, fireproofing techniques and the insurance of thatched properties. Further research is in progress on the life of thatching materials, the availability of reed, deterioration caused by nitrogen residues in the soil and all aspects of the craft. Everyone has been working together to secure the future of the thatching industry.

Soon, the majority of thatched houses will have passed into private hands and restoration will be complete. Barns will have been converted; already attention has been focused on ruined structures where hardly any stones are left standing. When these too have joined the ranks of desirable residences can there be a future for the thatcher and his thatch? Organic thatching materials can last a lifetime with interim maintenance. Could the time come when there are too many thatchers competing for the available work?

Efforts are being made to maintain a careful balance with just enough craftsmen for the work available. At present an open mind is being kept about the prospect of Continental thatchers tendering for work in Britain after 1992. Some fear the introduction of different thatching styles could destroy the vernacular that many thatchers have fought to preserve.

Today, over half of Britain's thatching reed is imported because many of the country's reed beds are in decline; a fact that saddens many thatchers who would gladly use Norfolk reed if it were available in large quantities. The British Reed Growers Association feels that, to date, little support has been given by central government to interest landowners in creating new reed beds.

Although there is no longer a danger that the thatcher will fade into obscurity, he has already had to change with the times and will have to continue to do so. Christopher White, the Chairman of the National Society of Master Thatchers sees 'a challenging future for the industry', for industry it has become, and is far removed from the rural craft of even 20 years ago.

Houses such as Court Farm at Glanvilles Wootton are harder to find in 1990. Round hedge poles that once supported a thick thatch are now visible.

Court Farm, Glanvilles Wootton, Dorset, 1989.

When the time comes for Court Farm to be restored there should be no reason to have the thatched roof replaced by alternative roofing materials

When it is restored, more substantial roof timbers may be covered with impervious felt, a flame-retardant insulation barrier may then be laid and the reed itself may be fireproofed. Perhaps a spark arrester will be fitted to the chimneypot as a final safety measure.

Many surplus farm cottages have been put on the market, but not all have been restored as well as Coombe Farm Cottages,

Dorset, where harmony has been retained by keeping the thatched roof. Less than 30 years ago the basic structure formed two farm cottages and modernization has only enhanced the overall effect.

The character of a barn can be lost once conversion is allowed, but this is often the only way to preserve the structure, for few are listed buildings. In some areas 80 per cent of barns have already been converted

167

Coombe Cottage, Coombe, Sherborne, Dorset.
Coombe Farm Cottages were sympathetically converted to one house, retaining the thatched roof

and many people are willing to pay a lot to own one.

The thatched tithe barn at Upminster in Essex, just a short distance from a London Underground station, has been given a new lease of life as a rural life museum, managed by the Hornchurch and District Historical Society. Member Fred Mead has furthered his interest in country crafts by forming a friendship with Dorset's oldest Master Thatcher, Simon Garrett, who has presented him with a collection of thatching tools, which were displayed at the museum in 1990.

Kent Master Thatcher Peter Brocklebank undertook a unique thatching assignment in 1989 for Trans Manche Link, completing the massive 320 square-foot roof of an

eighteenth-century barn in the village of Farthingloe, destined to be a study centre and chapel for Channel Tunnel workers.

Great Priory Barn, at Panfield, Essex has a new use today. In 1986 it became the centre for an antique restoration business, and a large number of organizations were involved in the project, including local and central government grant-giving supervisory agencies, private contractors and craftsmen. Financial support came from English Heritage and technical guidance from county council conservation officers. Thatching advice was given by the Rural Development Commission and a local Essex thatcher reproduced the rare, traditional, tiled valley between the thatched roofs.

Barn conversions are not just a whim of

recent years. In 1939, the fifteenth-century Barton House at Newton, Dorset, once given to Catherine Parr (the last wife of Henry VIII), was being doubled in size. The barn attached to the house was having doors and windows inserted and windows were added to the upper storey at the rear of the house. While the builders worked from their wooden scaffolding, two thatchers worked on the new and complex roof to replace long straw with a sleeker covering of combed wheat reed. Great skill was required to form a pleasing coat around the many new dormer windows.

Not all barns have become domestic dwellings. Fourteenth-century Chesterfield tithe barn was converted into a new free house and restaurant in 1989 and the roof was thatched by Peter Brocklebank.

Until recently thatch was considered a fire risk and thus insurance premiums were high. Specialist firms now offer more competitive rates achieved by careful risk management, monitoring of claims, liaison with craftsmen and making available advice to their clients. Marsh reed, being less combustible, will sometimes be treated more favourably. Preventative measures and common sense can prevent major disasters but sometimes the cause of fires can be attributed to electrical faults, blow-lamps, fireworks, sparks from a badly sited bonfire or even a carelessly wielded welding torch.

The Cott Inn at Dartington, Devon is reputed to be the second oldest inn in Britain and, in 1961, was the frontispiece of the Rural Industries Bureau's book *The Thatcher's Craft* when it had just been

Converted barn at Muchelney, Somerset.

Conversion is sometimes the only option for a large barn but once windows have been inserted its character may well be lost for ever

The Cott Inn, Dartington, Devon.

Fire can still devastate thatched properties, but preventative measures will be taken when the Cott Inn is rebuilt

thatched in Abbotsbury marsh reed; but in August 1989 disaster struck and 13 people had to be rescued by firemen. The blaze was probably started by an electrical fault.

During the severe winter of 1962 Woolston House, Somerset, with one of the largest thatched roofs in the area and fine verandahs, was destroyed when a blow-lamp was used in the roof space to defrost frozen pipes. The whole estate was surrounded by a thatched wall.

From the Middle Ages, methods of fireproofing thatch have been debated. Once upon a time it was common to daub thatch with a plaster mixture. More recently,

chemical dips have been tried with limited long-term success and sparge-pipes (sprinklers) have been fixed to the ridges of cottages to provide a waterfall in case of fire. Barrier methods are now being introduced and some are at an experimental stage. Diss Ironworks, a small family firm in Norfolk, received a request to produce a spark arrester by one new thatch owner who could not insure his property unless one was fitted to his chimney stack. No firm appeared to make them, although some owners had resorted to placing crumpled balls of small-gauge wire into the pot. Diss Ironworks produced prototypes in a galvanized finish, followed by stainless steel models to suit all fuels, and now despatch four spark arresters a week to meet the growing demand.

The younger generation of craftsmen that was needed to cope with the increased demand for thatch did not always come from established thatching families. The importance of providing a standard training programme was realized by the Rural Development Commission (RDC) who launched an apprenticeship scheme 25 years ago. Ten apprentices are accepted annually, providing they have already obtained places with thatchers in their area, as experience can only be gained from working on a wide variety of roof styles. Residential periods are spent at Knuston Hall, Northamptonshire

where practice roofs are available and courses include estimating, knowledge of materials, accounts and VAT. By limiting the number of apprentices the RDC feels the correct balance can be maintained.

Although the thatching industry is enjoying a revival, the time must come when thatched cottages have been restored, extensions have been completed and new work will only come from fresh developments. It would be sad if waning interest forced too many disillusioned young thatchers to abandon their craft because there was insufficient work.

The 25th year of apprenticeship training for thatchers was commemorated by the building of an ornamental thatched pagoda

Knuston Hall, Northants, provides formal training for thatching apprentices.

Practice roofs help the Rural Development Commission to train ten apprentice thatchers annually

A permanent reminder of 25 years of apprentice training at Knuston Hall, Northants.

An ornamental thatched pagoda was built in 1989 to commemorate the twenty-fifth year of the Rural Development Commission's apprentice training programme. During these 25 years the number of thatchers in Great Britain has doubled and the average age has fallen dramatically – a good omen for the future

in the grounds of Knuston Hall in 1989. This was an important event, for when the scheme started young thatchers were rare.

The Thatching Advisory Service also operates a training programme for prospective thatchers. In 1988 their first woman apprentice joined her tutor, Master Thatcher Mark Weber. Kate Glover was realizing the ambition she had had since she was ten years old and now at the age of 22 she is already a competent thatcher. Her tutor says she has the making of a fine

thatcher, with an excellent eye for balance and the right attitude towards her work. Kate Glover is not the first woman thatcher, for almost 30 years ago two daughters of the Martin family of Dorset Master Thatchers learnt the craft. In 1971 Annie Maltin, a student at Dartington College of Arts, spent her vacations working with thatcher Brian Whitemore of Ash Priors, Somerset. A few years later 16-year-old Janet Sansom became apprentice to thatcher Eric Streeter on the Isle of Wight. In 1990 women

This woman thatcher is not unique.

Kate Glover became the Thatching Advisory Service's first woman thatcher in 1988. Other women thatchers are working in Dorset and Devon in 1990

thatchers are also at work in Dorset and Devon.

Many thatchers showed artistic flair at school. Dan Munro knew before he left school in 1986 that he wanted to become a thatcher. Others, like Tony Cottrell of Wimborne, Dorset, turned to thatching after trying other occupations first. He was a baker, and artist, and when work was in short supply as a freelance artist, he accepted an offer to help a thatcher friend. He found the outdoor life and the opportunity to express his artistic talent on everchanging roof styles suited him and he has now been thatching for 16 years.

Today, a number of Poles are working for franchise thatchers throughout the country. George Jedyinski thatched a summerhouse with Kate Glover at Claygate Master Thatchers Shop, and Janek, from Suwalki (a forest region near the Russian border), joined thatcher Richard Yeo in Devon and proved to be an excellent and fast thatcher using about 110 bundles of reed a day compared with the more usual 65! Some British thatchers find work abroad. Arthur Farman visited Holland and France to thatch early this century, and thatcher Harold Wright's first apprentice in Somerset 15 years ago now lives and thatches in Normandy, France.

In 1989 thatcher Kit Davis of Oxfordshire moved his office to a thatched pavilion at one of the five Master Thatchers shops, at a garden centre at Frilford, near Abingdon. A

Thatch in 1990 adorns a wide variety of structures in all shapes and sizes.

The Thatching Advisory Service helps to promote the many uses of thatch. There is no need to live in a thatched property to appreciate the materials, for thatched bird-tables, dovecots, summerhouses and offices are but a few of the items available, as well as a comprehensive advice service

wide variety of small gifts including thatched nest-boxes, bird-tables and corn dollies is available, as well as larger thatched summerhouses and pavilions. Thatched tiles have recently been introduced and are already decorating the rhino houses at Windsor Safari Park while in Hampshire they provide the canopies in Bordon Market.

Agricultural shows often provided an opportunity for people to see a thatcher at work. Thatcher Harold Wright from Compton Dundon, Somerset demonstrated his craft for the 25th year in 1989 at the Royal Bath and West Show. Until recently, the demonstration rick played as important a part as the demonstration roof, for it helped keep the tradition of rick thatching alive. In 1990 the picture is changing and more ricks are being built in farmers' fields.

Montague Davis is also well known at the Royal Bath and West Show where he demonstrates hurdle-making. At Milborne St Andrew he also makes spars. His brother, Sidney Donald Davis, can be seen at the Milton Abbas village Open Day and in 1989 took a large party of primary school pupils to his hazel coppice. For some children it was their first visit to an ancient woodland and they recorded their vivid and lasting impressions in letters of thanks. The Davis family have also supplied hurdles and materials for reconstructed settlements at Coalville, Leicestershire and at Grimsby but sadly both have been vandalized and replacement materials are now required.

The RSPB (Royal Society for the Protection of Birds) Reserve Centre at Radipole, Dorset was built at a time when no-one wanted a licence to cut their marsh reed and all such rights passed to the RSPB. The building was thatched with Norfolk reed. Today the picture has improved, and a small commercial reed bed within the reserve is cut by hand, producing about a thousand bundles of reed annually. The

Hurdlemaker Montague Davis from Milborne St Andrew, Dorset, is a popular figure at the Royal Bath and West Show, 1989.

Woodland crafts are rarely appreciated by members of the public as the hurdlemaker and sparmaker work in inaccessible places. Demonstrations help to establish an awareness that the craft is still alive today. Montague Davis is well-known craftsman at the Royal Bath and West Show

The Royal Bath and West Show provides the opportunity for a thatcher to talk to an appreciative audience at ground level.

A chance to see the tools and materials and talk to a thatcher can only help increase awareness of his craft and so help secure its future. Harold Wright demonstrated his craft at the Royal Bath and West Show for the twenth-fifth year in 1989

1986 to 1988 harvests supplied reed to Cranborne Middle School for their replica Iron Age settlement and the 1989 harvest was used for screening purposes by the RSPB on the reserve site. The 1990 harvest will supply reed for Puddletown Middle School's replica Saxon longhouse that now has planning permission.

Not everyone wishes to live in an old cottage and today new thatched houses are built. Fairclough Homes's mixed estate at Formby, Merseyside advertised 'a rare and

177

Radipole, near Weymouth, Dorset.

The RSPB Reserve Centre at Radipole Lake, Dorset marks the turning point for the thatcher and his thatch. Labour was unavailable to cut the 3,000 bundles of reed needed for the roof in 1982 and, instead, reed was brought from Hickling Broad, Norfolk. Today, the commercial reed beds are being cut again with the remaining reed managed specifically for wildlife

exquisite opportunity in new residential property'. Unlike thatched houses of the past these properties have double glazing, cavity walls and loft insulation. The houses, thatched by John Burke of Cheshire, proved so popular that another development is planned for Hartford in Cheshire. Five houses on Balfour Beatty's Brackenfield Chase development near Thurcaston, Leicester were thatched in water reed with combed wheat-reed ridges by Peter Brugge and Master Thatchers North. The houses attracted a great deal of interest and were filmed by the BBC for their *Country File* programme. Balfour Beatty's other development of thatched houses at Chineham, Hampshire attracted an equal amount of publicity.

For some builders and architects it is their first encounter with thatch on new house construction and a number of seminars have been organized by the Thatching Advisory Service covering the specific requirements needed for all aspects of thatch.

Ten thatchers spent three days thatching a huge medieval farmhouse reconstruction for BBC Television Bristol's *Precious Bane* production. The work would normally have taken almost two months to complete! Other thatchers have accepted thatching assignments in America and Canada.

However much the new thatched roof is appreciated, and help and encouragement given to train a new generation of Master Thatchers, care must be taken to ensure a steady supply of materials for the future. Not only must there be plentiful supplies of thatching reed but also spars. An appreciation of hazel cannot start too soon. At the age of three, Simon planted his first hazel nuts. By the age of six years he had found good homes for his trees in

Abbots Mede, Formby, Merseyside.

A mixture of styles is acceptable today and thatch stands next to tiles on this executive estate, built by Fairclough Homes Ltd in 1989. The houses proved so popular that more are now being built

Hampshire, Wiltshire, Dorset, Somerset and Kent. Now his ambition is to plant a hazel coppice for the twenty-first century. Thatching reed in a good season will give an immediate profit, but hazel will only realize its first cash crop after a minimum of seven years, and possibly even longer on poorer soil. The hazel provides a natural habitat that is appreciated by flowers, wildlife – and man.

Henry Abbey (1842–1911) ended his poem 'Planting Trees' with the line: 'We plant the house when we plant the tree.' Timber provides rafters, floorboards, doors, windows and the thatching spars but until the time comes when young men show an interest in becoming hurdle- and sparmakers, and not just thatchers, the future of the underwood must remain uncertain.

Simon Nash grows trees for future generations to enjoy, and hazel to help secure a future for the sparmaker.

It is important to ensure an adequate supply of spars as well as reed. At three years of age, Simon's hazel is already showing its multi-branching tendencies and has a well-developed root system. Simon hopes to plant a new coppice when he is older, as he appreciates the value of the humble hazel

Glossary

A short list of common thatching terms; many more, including countless regional variations, are also still in existence.

Abbotsbury reed: marsh or water reed grown at Abbotsbury, Dorset, locally known as 'spear'

Apron: *see* Skirts

Backfill: a thin layer of thatch laid over the battens on a new roof to enable further courses to be laid without catching on the timber

Barge: *see* Gable

Barge-board: a piece of timber, sometimes decoratively carved, following the line of thatch at the gable end to cover the ends of the horizontal roof timbers

Base coat: a clean layer of original thatch on which the new thatch will be laid

Bat: *see* Leggett

Batten: a small horizontal strip of wood onto which a new thatched coat is attached

Bed: a prepared heap of long straw, sedge or rye which, after wetting, will be drawn or bundled into yealms

Beetle: regional variations include beadle, *see* Leggett

Biddle: a short roof-ladder fixed into the roof with spikes, either two-runged or with several rungs

Binders: *see* Sways

Bottles: small tightly tied bundles also known as eaves, bundles, or wads, inserted to form the eaves

Broaches: *see* Spars

Brotches: *see* Spars

Brow: *see* Gable

Brow course: the course above the eaves bundles

Bunch: bundle of water reed approximately 24 inches (60 centimetres) in circumference. Can be as big as 3 feet (1 metre)

Capping: *see* Ridge

Catslide roof: one slope covering the main roof and an extension

Coat: the whole thatched roof visible to the eye

Combed wheat reed: wheat straw that has been passed through a reed comber

Cord: *see* Tarred twine

Course: a horizontal layer of reed or straw thatch laid along the roof

Crooks: iron or steel hooked rods pointed at one end and used with a sway or metal rod to fix the thatch to the rafters

Cross spars: split strips of spar material used in a decorative manner at the ridge

Crucks: large, wooden timbers selected to make the frame used in medieval house-building, where the timbers run from roof apex to ground level

Devon reed: Combed wheat reed

Dolly: *see* Roll

Dormer: a projecting roof window with a roof of its own

Dresser: *see* Leggett

Dutchman: a rounded, wooden tool used for forming valleys in the thatch. Similar in size to the leggett

Eaves: the horizontal overhang of a roof projecting beyond the face of a wall

Eaves bundles: *see* Bottles

Eaves hook: tool used for cutting the eaves to shape

Eaves knife: *see* Eaves hook

Eaves wads: *see* Bottles

Fathom: 6-foot (1.8-metre) circumference bundle of Norfolk reed made up of six ordinary bundles laid together

Fillet: *see* Flashing

Flashing: sheet-lead fitting over thatch and into brickwork at junction with chimney. Can be made of cement

Fleeking: a woven mat of water reed used in place of battens, often decorative where rafters are exposed

Flue: *see* Gable

Gable: the vertical triangular wall at the end of the roof. Also the finished edge of thatch overhanging the gable, alternatively known as 'flue', 'verge' or 'barge'

Gads: bundles of hazel or willow, copsed and trimmed to size ready to be made into spars

Hip: the sloping external intersection of two inclined roof surfaces

Hooks: *see* Crooks

Hovers knive: Long-handled gable/barge knife with a long blade

Ledgers: *see* Sways

Leggett: also known as a beetle. A grooved, square, wooden-headed tool on a handle used for dressing combed wheat reed or water reed into place

Liggers or **Rods:** long lengths of split hazel or willow, used on the outside surface of ridges, eaves and gables

Long straw: threshed wheat straw, wetted and prepared by hand

Marsh reed: *see* Water reed

Nails: *see* Crooks

Needle: a straight or curved, eyed needle made of metal, flat on one side for sewing base coat of thatch onto the battens

Nitch: a bundle of combed wheat reed weighing approximately 29 lb (13 kg)

Norfolk reed: water reed grown in Norfolk and the surrounding counties. *See* Water reed

Outshut: an extension of a building under a lean-to roof

Patterned ridge: decorated ridge with scallops, points or other shapes cut into the sedge or straw ridge

Pinnacle: raised end of ridge at gable, formed into a peak

Rafter: one of several timbers supporting the roof covering

Ridge: the apex of a roof protected by an additional layer of sedge or straw, often decoratively cut

Ridge roll: *see* Roll

Rods: *see* Liggers.

Roll: sometimes called dolly. Bundle of reed or straw used for building up ridge prior to capping

Rye straw: straw threshed and used for ridging

Sedge: used for the ridge capping on water-reed thatch

Shearing hook: hook used to give the thatch its final look, by trimming protruding ends

Skirts: the layer of thatch under windows or chimneys, or completing a block-cut ridge, fixed with spars and liggers

Spar hook: a small, very sharp, billhook used for all aspects of sparmaking

Spars: split hazel or willow rods pointed at each end and twisted in the centre to form a staple. Used for securing new coat of thatch to existing coat, also to secure liggers on ridges. Countless regional names exist

Spear: regional name for Abbotsbury marsh or water reed

Spicks: *see* Spars

Spikes: *see* Crooks

Spitts: *see* Spars

Sprays: *see* Spars

Staples: *see* Spars

Stool: hazel cut back to the roots to encourage spar growth

Straw bond: a straw rope twisted with a whimble and fixed with spars. Often used in rick thatching

Stulch: a strip of thatch running from eaves to ridge, laid as work proceeds

Sways: sometimes called ledgers or binders. Split or round rods used to secure thatch to roof by being placed horizontally across each course of thatch and covered by each succeeding course

Tallet: a room above the stable, often reached by an outside ladder, used for storing fodder, harness and even as accommodation by the poorer servants

Tarred twine: strong cord treated with Stockholm tar, and used for stitching thatch to rafters or battens. Also called tarline

Throw-hook: *see* Wimble

Valley: the sloping internal junction of two inclined roof surfaces

Verge: *see* Gable

Water reed: reed grown on British and Continental marshes and riverside marshland; sometimes contains a small amount of mace reed and other marginal plants

Wimble: also known as whimmer, whimble or wink and used for making a straw rope. A shaped piece of round iron, often home-made, with a crook at one end into which is inserted a loop of straw, with one handle in the middle and another at the end. The wimble is rotated to twist the straw

Yealm: a prepared, drawn layer of wet straw or sedge, sometimes called helm

Yealm holder: forked hazel stick made into a hod to carry yealms onto the roof

Chapter notes

A great deal of the information for this book has been gained from conversations with Master Thatchers and their apprentices, hurdlemakers, sparmakers, and farmers and their relations. Access has been given to privately held collections of papers, notes and account books that are not deposited in public offices.

Excerpts from newspapers have been reproduced by permission of the Western Gazette Co Ltd, Yeovil.

1. *A craft is born* (p. 12)

1 Rev. John Hutchins, *The History & Antiquities of the County of Dorset*, Vol. 2, p. 119
2 T. Hudson Turner, *Some Account of Domestic Architecture in England*, 1. (J.H. Parke, 1851)
3 *Bishop Hall's Satires*, *c*. 1610, Bk. V, 'Satire' (i)
4 Information on the London theatres kindly supplied by Pentagram Design Ltd, London
5 Hampshire Record Office, *Expenses in the New Assart* [1251/2] *Downton, Wilts*. (MS Eccl. Comm 2/159447), from an account roll of the Bishopric of Winchester
6 D. Wills, *The Estate Book of Henry de Bray of Northamptonshire*, pp. 49–51, Camden Soc. 1916
7 *Western Daily Press*, 20 March 1989, pp. 18–19
8 'Thatching on the Isle of Man', produced and kindly supplied with additional material by the Manx Museum
9 Ibid.

2. *The thatcher's thatch* (p. 32)

1 *Daily Mail*, 13 March 1972
2 Jonathan MacDonald, curator and owner of the Museum of Island Life, Skye
3 Simon Garrett's *Account Book* (1957–67). Private Coll.
4 *Western Flying Post & Sherborne Mercury*, 6 April 1789
5 *Western Flying Post & Sherborne Mercury*, 1 December 1830
6 A. Pearman, *Dorset Year Book 1953/4*, 'Of Rural Industries', pp. 145–6
7 Sherborne Museum, *Thatching Bill* of Edward Freke

3. *The spar* (p. 56)

1 Dorset County Record Office, *Notes on Materials and Costs*, (DR D 449/3 p. 61) in a book of Henry Conway of Evershot, builder, 1876
2 J. Fowler, *Mediaeval Sherborne*, pp. 198–9, (Longmans, 1951) and in a conversation between the author and thatcher Simon Garrett prior to publication
3 *As* **1**
4 Dorset County Record Office, Share MSS: ledger of William Garrett of Trent, thatcher, 1847–89 (D 200/2)
5 Ibid.
6 Crown Copyright, reprod. by permission of the Forestry Commission, *FC Bulletin 27*,

W.G. Trust: 'The Hazel Underwood Industry' pp. 7–11

7   Crown Copyright reprod. by permission of the Forestry Commission, *FC Bulletin 62*, J. Evans: 'Silviculture of Broadleaved Woodlands 1984'

4. *House and home* (p. 75)

1   Hayward N. & Windridge N., *Badges & Beans*, Hundred of Yetminster History Soc., 1989
2   L. Weaver, *Country Life Book of Cottages*, 2nd ed., published by *Country Life* 1919, pp. 87–92, 151–2, 232–4
3   Ibid.
4   Ibid.
5   *Dorset Year Book 1930*
6   A. Pearman, *Dorset Year Book 1953/4*, 'Of Rural Industries', pp. 144–6
7   Dorset County Record Office: Share MSS: ledger of William Garrett of Trent, thatcher, 1847–89 (D 200/2)

5. *The farm* (p. 97)

1   E.J. Stowe, *Thatching of Rick and Barn*, Landsmans Library, 1954
2   Dorset County Record Office: Share MSS: ledger of William Garrett of Trent, thatcher, 1847–89 (D 200/2)
3   Ibid.
4   Simon Garrett's 'Account Book' (1956–66), private coll.

5   *As* **2**
6   Ibid.
7   Ibid.
8   Ibid.
9   Ibid.
10 Ibid.

6. *Cottage orné* (p. 120)

1   R. Carew, *Survey of Cornwall*, 1692, p. 66
2   C. Fiennes, *Journey*, 1700, ed. C. Morris, 1947, p. 51
3   British Parliamentary Paper (BPP), 1865, XXIV, pp. 148–51
4   Ibid.

7. *Thatcher – the man* (p. 144)

1   *Anno Quinto Elizabethae*, Cap 4, 1562
2   Thornford School, 'Minute Book', 1865–90
3   Dorset County Record Office: Share MSS: ledger of William Garrett of Trent, thatcher, 1847–89, (D 200/2)
4   Rev E.C. Powell, *Notes on East Coker*, private publication
5   Flora Thompson, *The Peveral Papers*, Century Hutchinson Ltd, 1986, p. 88
6   R. Guttridge, *Dorset Smugglers*, Dorset Publishing Co., 1984
7   A. Pearman, *Dorset Year Book 1953/4*, 'Of Rural Industries', pp. 144–6
8   Crown Copyright, reprod. with the permission of the Controller of HMSO

Select reading list

Abbott, Mike, *Green Woodwork – working with wood the natural way* (Guild of Master Craftsmen, 1989)

Billett, Michael, *Thatch and Thatched Buildings* (Hale, 1979)

Billett, Michael, *Thatched Buildings of Dorset* (Hale, 1984)

Brown, Jonathan, *Farm Machinery 1750–1945* (Batsford, 1989)

Brown, R.J., *The English Country Cottage* (Hale, 1979)

Condry, William, *Woodlands*, (William Collins, 1974)

Council for Small Industries in Rural Areas, *The Thatcher's Craft* (RIB, 1960)

Edlin, Herbert L., *Woodland Crafts of Britain* (David & Charles, 1973)

Evans, J., *Silviculture of Broadleaved Woodland*, Forestry Commission Bulletin 62 (1984)

Fearn, Jaqueline, *Thatch and Thatching* (Shire Publications, 1976)

Fussell, G.E., *The Farmer's Tools* (Bloomsbury Books, 1985)

Hall, Nicolas, *Thatching: a handbook* (Intermediate Technology Publications, 1988)

Innocent, C.F., *The Development of English Building Construction* (Cambridge University Press, 1975)

Lambeth, Minnie, *A Golden Dolly* (Baker, 1973)

Manners, J.E., *Country Crafts Today* (David & Charles, 1974)

Robinson J.M., *Georgian Model Farms* (Clarendon Press, 1984)

Staniforth, Arthur, *Straw and Straw Craftsmen* (Shire Publications, 1981)

Weaver, Lawrence, *The Country Life Book of Cottages* (Country Life, 2nd ed. 1919)

West, Robert C., *Thatch – a manual for owners, surveyors, architects and builders* (David & Charles, 1987)

Further reading

Brockett, Peter, & Wright, Adela, 'The Care and Repair of Thatched Roofs', Technical Pamphlet 10. S.P.A.B. and CoSira. (Eyre & Spottiswoode, 1986)

Clark, C., 'Thatch, thatchers and thatching', *Agricultural Journal*, Vol. 53 (London, January 1947)

Crowther, R.E. & Evans, J. 'Coppice', Forestry Commission leaflet 83, (HMSO, 1984)

Darby, K., 'Thatch as a modern building material' *Architects' Journal* (London, September 1986)

Hall, N.L., 'Has thatch a future?' *Appropriate Technology* Vol. 8. No. 3 (London, 1981)

Haslam, S.M., 'The Reed' ('Norfolk Reed'), Norfolk Reed Growers' Assn., 2nd. ed. (1972)

National Council of Master Thatchers Information Pack ('Fire retardation, performance of thatch, roof construction, extending thatched properties') (NCMTA, 1990)

Stowe, E.J., 'Thatching of Rick and Barn', (Landsmans Library, 1954)

Thatching Advisory Service Ltd, 'Insuring Thatch'

Thatching Advisory Service Ltd, 'Patching and Re-thatching'

Thatching Advisory Service Ltd, 'Specifications on Thatch'

Thatching Advisory Service Ltd, *Thatch* (a quarterly magazine)

White, J.E.J. 'Hazel Coppice at Westonbirt', (Forestry Commission, 1981)

Useful
addresses

The following select list of addresses can provide further information on all aspects of the thatcher's craft.

Thatch

The British Reed Growers Association
Francis Hornor & Son
Old Bank of England Court
Queen Street
Norwich NR2 4TA

Abbotsbury Reed
Publicity Officer
Abbotsbury Swannery
Abbotsbury
Dorset

Peter Grimley
Reed Importer
Thorne Farm New Bungalow
Cheriton Bishop
Nr Okehampton
Devon

Thatchers and thatching careers

National Council of Master Thatchers
    Associations
The Lane
Rushall
Pusey
Wiltshire
SN9 6EN

National Society of Master Thatchers
Hi-view
Little Street
Yardley Hastings
Northampton

Rural Development Commission
(formerly CoSira & RIB)
141 Castle Street
Salisbury
Wiltshire SP1 3TP

Thatching Advisory Services Ltd
Rose Tree Farm
29 Nine Mile Ride
Finchampstead
Wokingham
Berkshire RG11 4QD

Thatch protection

Double Shield Spark Arresters
Diss Ironworks
Hyde Engineering
Norfolk House
St Nicholas Street
Diss
Norfolk

Thatch Owners Insurance Agency Ltd
4 Mount Mews
High Street
Hampton
Middlesex TW12 2SH

Thatching Advisory Service (Insurance) Ltd
(*as above*)

Protection and appreciation of ancient buildings

SPAB
The Society for the Protection of Ancient
    Buildings
37 Spital Square,
London E1 6DY

Tel. 071 377 1644

The Landmark Trust
Shottesbrooke
Maidenhead
Berkshire SL6 3SW

Tel. 062 882 5925

Coppice management

The Forestry Commission
Forest Research Station
Alice Holt Lodge
Wrecclesham
Farnham
Surrey GU10 4LH

Sparmaking

Graeme Coombs
The Bungalow
King Stag
Nr Sturminster Newton
Dorset

Hurdle-making

M. & S. Davis
Milborne St Andrew
Nr Dorchester
Dorset

Reed management for the wildlife habitat

RSPB Warden
The Lodge & Information Centre
Radipole Lake Nature Reserve
Radipole
Weymouth
Dorset

The Swanherd
Abbotsbury Swannery
Abbotsbury
Dorset

Thatched buildings and rural life museums

Butser Ancient Farm Project Trust,
The Queen Elizabeth Country Park Centre
Gravel Hill
Horndean
Portsmouth
Hampshire PO8 OQE

Jonathan MacDonald
Skye Museum of Island Life
Isle of Skye
Scotland

The Weald & Downland Open Air Museum
Singleton
Chichester
Sussex PO18 OEU

The Welsh Folk Museum
St Fagans
Cardiff CF5 6XB

Thie Tashtee Vannin
The Manx Museum
Cregneash Village Folk Museum
Douglas
Isle of Man

Index